Negotiation

The Harvard Business Essentials Series

The Harvard Business Essentials series is designed to provide comprehensive advice, personal coaching, background information, and guidance on the most relevant topics in business. Drawing on rich content from Harvard Business School Publishing and other sources, these concise guides are carefully crafted to provide a highly practical resource for readers with all levels of experience. To assure quality and accuracy, each volume is closely reviewed by a specialized content adviser from a world-class business school. Whether you are a new manager interested in expanding your skills or an experienced executive looking for a personal resource, these solution-oriented books offer reliable answers at your fingertips.

Other books in the series:

Finance for Managers
Hiring and Keeping the Best People
Managing Change and Transition
Business Communication
Managing Creativity and Innovation

Negotiation

Harvard Business School Press | *Boston, Massachusetts*

No part of this publication may be reproduced, stored in or introduced into a retrieval
system, or transmitted, in any form, or by any means (electronic, mechanical, photo-
copying, recording, or otherwise), without the prior permission of the publisher.
Requests for permission should be directed to permissions@hbsp.harvard.edu,
or mailed to Permissions, Harvard Business School Publishing,
60 Harvard Way, Boston, Massachusetts 02163.

978-1-59139-111-1 (ISBN 13)

Library of Congress Cataloging-in-Publication Data
Harvard business essentials : negotiation
p. cm. — (The Harvard business essentials series)
Includes bibliographical references and index.
ISBN 1-59139-111-3
1. Negotiation in business. I. Series.
HD58.6.H3828 2003
2003009818

Contents

Negotiation

Introduction

Negotiation is the means by which people deal with their differences. Whether those differences involve the purchase of a new automobile, a labor contract dispute, the terms of a sale, a complex alliance between two companies, or a peace accord between warring nations, resolutions are typically sought through negotiations. To negotiate is to seek mutual agreement through dialogue.

Negotiation is an ever-present feature of our lives both at home and at work. When a parent and a child talk about how the child will improve his math scores, they are negotiating. So, too, are two spouses when they agree on who will do the yard work and who will do the grocery shopping this weekend. In the workplace, negotiations are even more ubiquitous. Indeed, the Latin root of the word (*negotiatus*) means "to carry on business." In modern Spanish, *negocios* means "business."

A business negotiation may be a formal affair that takes place across the proverbial bargaining table, in which you haggle over price and performance or the complex terms of a partnership venture. Alternatively, it may be much less formal, such as a meeting between you and several fellow employees whose collaboration is needed to get a job done. If you are a supervisor, manager, or executive, you probably spend a good part of your day negotiating with people inside or outside your organization—often without even realizing it. Whether you're closing a sale or getting a subordinate to agree to certain performance goals, you are negotiating.

Given the role of negotiations in our personal and professional lives, it's important to improve our negotiating skills. Even a modest improvement in those skills can yield a sizable payoff, such as a larger pay raise, a better deal on a home purchase, or more effective working arrangements in the office. This book can help you improve your skills and make you a more effective negotiator.

Drawing on the best available literature in the field, *Harvard Business Essentials: Negotiation* explains the basic concepts followed by expert negotiators and creative problem solvers. It is packed with practical tips and examples that will help you in your personal life and in your career.

What's Ahead

Chapter 1 explains the basic types of negotiations: the distributive negotiation and the integrative deal. In the first, the value available to the parties is essentially fixed, and each seeks to claim as much of it as possible. Here, one party's gain comes at the expense of the others. This type is the so-called zero-sum game. In the second, the parties apply creativity and information sharing to create greater value for eventual distribution.

Chapter 2 moves from negotiation types to four concepts that every negotiator should understand and know how to apply: the BATNA, or best alternative to a negotiated agreement; the reservation price, the point at which you plan to walk away; the ZOPA, or zone of possible agreement in which a deal is feasible; and the value created through trades. Each of these concepts is explained and supported with examples.

Chapter 3 is about preparation. You should never enter a negotiation cold; instead, first learn as much as possible about your own interests and positions and those of the other side. You can prepare yourself using the steps offered in this chapter.

Once you've learned the basics and know what's needed for preparation, you're ready for chapter 4—"Table Tactics." This chapter shows you how to get the other side to the table, how to get negotiations off to a good start, and how to play the game, no matter which type of negotiation is involved. Here you'll learn about techniques such as anchoring and framing, and how you can some-times alter the negotiation process in your favor. Chapter 5 contin-ues that discussion with answers to frequently asked questions about negotiating tactics.

Not every negotiation goes smoothly—even those that involve friendly parties. One or more barriers—such as structural impedi-ments, lack of trust, and poor communication—can get in the way of a successful deal. Chapter 6 identifies these barriers and indicates how you can avoid them. Chapter 7 discusses mental errors that ne-gotiators sometime bring to the table. These include overconfidence, irrational expectations, and the tendency to escalate offers in an ego-driven zeal to win. Again, the chapter explains how you can avoid making these errors.

Chapter 8 is concerned with relationships. In a onetime trans-action, one's future relationships with the other parties do not mat-ter. The goal is to claim as much value as possible. The purchase of a rug from a street vendor is a typical example. But many personal and business deals involve multiple transactions over time among parties who seek to maintain productive relationships. These deals involve both tangible values and relationship values. Chapter 8 shows you how to maneuver in this tricky terrain and how you can separate deal val-ues from relationship values.

Chapter 9 is about negotiating for others. In many cases the people doing the actual bargaining are independent or employee agents of the respective parties: a lawyer representing a person bring-ing a personal injury suit, a purchasing manager representing his or her company in a supplier agreement, a union negotiator represent-ing a local unit in a dispute with a particular employer. There are often very good reasons to employ an agent in negotiations, as the chapter explains, but doing so generally opens the door to principal/agent conflicts. The chapter examines these conflicts and how they can be avoided or minimized.

It is obviously important for individuals to develop their negoti-ating skills. But what about organizations? Chapter 10 advances the idea of developing negotiating skill as an organizational competence. Imagine what your organization could achieve if its salespeople, supervisors, managers, and executives were to become progressively better negotiators. This chapter brings together two powerful concepts, continuous improvement and core competencies, to demonstrate how training, learning, and the reuse of learning can be applied to the development of negotiating skills.

Harvard Business Essentials: Negotiation contains several supplements. The first is an appendix containing worksheets that you may find helpful. Free interactive versions of these worksheets, as well as other tools found in this book and in other volumes of the series, are available and can be downloaded from the official Harvard Business Essentials Web site, www.elearning.hbsp.org/businesstools. The second supplement is a glossary of terms. Every discipline has its special vocabulary, and negotiating is no exception. When you see a word italicized in the text, that's your cue that the word is defined in the glossary. Finally, "For Further Reading" identifies books and articles that can tell you more about topics covered in this book. If you want to learn more, these publications can help you.

1

Types of Negotiation

Many Paths to a Deal

Key Topics Covered in This Chapter

- *Distributive negotiation: claiming value*

- *Integrative negotiation: creating and claiming value*

- *The negotiator's dilemma: trying to determine which game to play*

- *Multiphase and multiparty negotiations*

THERE ARE TWO primary kinds of negotiation. Chances are you have been involved in both at one time or another:

- **Distributive:** A negotiation in which the parties compete over the distribution of a fixed sum of value. The key question in a distributed negotiation is "Who will claim the most value?" In distributive negotiations, a gain by one side is made at the expense of the other.

- **Integrative:** A negotiation in which the parties cooperate to achieve maximum benefits by integrating their interests into an agreement. These deals are about creating value and claiming it.

Few of your negotiations will be purely distributive. Although direct competition between the interests and goals of negotiating parties is commonplace, opportunities to integrate the parties' interests and preferences usually exist. But for the purposes of pedagogy, this chapter examines each type in its pure form. These forms are complicated by two other facts of life addressed at the end of the chapter: Negotiations often take place in phases and may involve multiple parties.

Distributive Negotiation

The issue in a distributive negotiation is who will claim the most value. Some people refer to this type of negotiation as *zero-sum* or

zero-sum game [handwritten marginal note]

constant-sum negotiation. The term *win-lose* is probably more representative of what's involved. Classic examples include the following:

- The sale of a carpet, where the buyer and the seller do not know one another. There is no relationship; all that matters is the price, and each side haggles for the best deal. Every gain by one party represents a loss to the other.

- Wage negotiations between business owners and their union employees. The owners know that any amount conceded to the union will come out of their own pockets—and vice versa.

In a purely distributive negotiation, the value at stake is fixed, and each side's goal is to get as much of it as possible. Consider the example of two people negotiating over shares of a freshly baked apple pie. Each aims to negotiate for as large a portion of that pie as possible, knowing that any concession made to the other party will reduce his or her share by an equal amount. Or consider this typical business example:

> *Acme Manufacturing and a supplier, Best Parts Company, are negotiating an agreement under which Best Parts will make and deliver 10,000 specified widgets over a period of six months. Acme's purchasing manager has been instructed to get the lowest possible price, so she's pushing for $1.75 per widget. Best Parts's sales manager, on the other hand, is trying to maximize the price his employer receives; he's asking for $2.00 per widget. Neither is willing to discuss anything but price.*
>
> *In the end, Acme Manufacturing gets its price. With several potential sellers to turn to, its purchasing manager holds out until the other side, which lacks other sales outlets, caves in and takes $1.75 per widget.*

The seller's goal in a distributive deal is to negotiate as high a price as possible; the buyer's goal is to negotiate as low a price as possible. A dollar more to one side is a dollar less to the other. Thus, the seller and the buyer compete to claim the greatest possible value for themselves. There is a tug of war going on here. Each negotiator aims to "pull" the final deal point as close to his or her side's desired price as possible (or even beyond it).

Relationship and reputation mean little in this tug of war: The negotiators are not willing to trade value in the deal for value in their relationship with the other side. For example, a business executive being transferred to another metropolitan area is shopping for a house. She is not concerned with her long-term relationship with a home seller when she begins negotiating to purchase the seller's house. Chances are that the seller is a total stranger—and will remain so after the transaction takes place.

Information plays an important role in this type of negotiation. The less the other side knows about your weaknesses and real preferences, and the more it knows about your bargaining strength, the better will be your position. For example, the Best Parts sale manager would be unwise if he let the other side know that he had few other takers for his company's widgets, or that he was currently selling the same widgets to another manufacturer for less than $2 each. Conversely, Acme's buyer would be eager to let the other side know that other parts manufacturers are currently knocking on her door, each eager to get the business.

To achieve success in a distributive negotiation, remember the following:

- The first offer can become a strong psychological anchor point, one that sets the bargaining range. Studies show that negotiation outcomes often correlate with the first offer. So start at the right place.

- Do not disclose any significant information about your circumstances—including why you want to make a deal, your real interests or business constraints, your preferences among issues or options, or the point at which you'd walk away from the table. It is advantageous, however, to let the other side know that you have good options if this deal falls through.

- Information about the other side can benefit you. Learn as much as possible about the other side's circumstances and preferences—including why they want to make a deal, their real interests and business constraints, and their preferences among issues or options.

- Exploit what you learn about the other side in setting your first offer or demand.

- Don't overshoot. If you claim aggressively or greedily, the other side may walk away. You will have lost the opportunity to make a deal.

Integrative Negotiation

In an integrative negotiation, the parties cooperate to achieve maximum benefits by integrating their interests into an agreement while also competing to divide the value. In integrative negotiations you have to be good at both creating value and claiming it.

Consider the following typical business example of an integrative negotiation:

Gomez Electronics and one of its primary suppliers, Kraft Components Company, are negotiating an agreement under which Kraft will build and deliver 10,000 switches over a period of six months. Gomez is interested in getting the lowest possible price, but is likewise interested in maintaining a long-term relationship with Kraft, which has been an innovative and reliable supplier over the years. Kraft's sales manager would like to maximize the price his company receives under the contract, but must be mindful of the relationship. He'd hate to lose this long-term customer.

As long-term partners, each side is willing to disclose some of its interests to the other. That way, if one party must give ground on price, the other party might be able to offer value on some other front.

Together, the two negotiators settle on an agreement that gives Kraft what it wants: $2 per switch. But in return, Kraft agrees to give Gomez Electronics sixty days to pay instead of the usual thirty-day arrangement. The extra thirty-day float helps Gomez reduce its working capital requirements over the term of the agreement. Further, the two firms agree to collaborate in designing a new set of switches for a Gomez product currently on the drawing boards.

Examples like this one have become more and more commonplace on the manufacturer–supplier front as big companies shift their tactics from squeezing suppliers—and dealing with many of them through short-term transactions—to developing long-term relationships with just a handful of suppliers. In many of these cases, suppliers and original equipment manufacturers (OEMs) collaborate in areas of quality control and product development. The growing use of joint ventures and outsourcing has likewise motivated organizations to think more about relationships and less about winning what often appears to be a zero-sum game.

In an integrative negotiation, your task is twofold: (1) to create as much value as possible for you and for the other side, and (2) to claim value for yourself. Many use the term *win-win* in referring to this type of arrangement. Unfortunately, that term implies that all parties get everything they want, which is rarely the case. More likely, each makes trade-offs to get the things they value most, while giving up other, less critical factors. For example, in the manufacturer-supplier case just described, Kraft got the unit price it wanted, but gave ground to Gomez Electronics on payment terms.

Sometimes, the two sides' interests do not compete at all. In these cases the task is to arrive at a deal that integrates their interests as efficiently as possible. Agreeing to yield more of what one negotiator values does not necessarily require the other negotiator to take less of anything he or she values. Thus, the ability of one side to claim or win what it wants or needs in the deal does not necessarily detract from the other's ability to claim or win just as much.

There are often many items or issues to be negotiated in an integrated negotiation—not simply price, delivery date, or any other single issue. Indeed, opportunities for creativity abound.

Negotiation specialist Mark Gordon, who coined the term "collaborative bargaining" for this type of negotiation, says that the parties should look for creative options, and not focus on which concessions to make. "You have to believe that it's in your interest to look for ways to benefit your negotiating counterpart. Your goal is not to hurt them, but to help them at little cost to yourself—and have them help you at little cost to them. The more creative you are at coming up with things that are good for both of you the happier both of you will be."[1] This creativity is only possible if both parties understand their own key interests *and* the key interests of the other side.

Is Win-Win for Real?

Most books and training courses on negotiations use the term "win-win" to describe integrative deals. In fact, both the term and the concept have become so popular that they have become clichés: "We're looking for a win-win deal with our customers." "Here at ExploitCo, management and employees share a win-win attitude."

It all sounds very high-minded. Win-win resonates with our cultural belief that relationships should be mutually beneficial, not exploitive, one-sided, or coercive.

But not everyone is happy with the term. Author and negotiating consultant Jim Camp is an outspoken critic. To him, win-win is a sucker's game, and more likely to be a losing game for the unwary:

> [S]hrewd negotiators in every field understand that a gung ho, win-win negotiator on the other side of the table is a sitting duck. . . . Those smooth-talking negotiators don't compromise, but they demand that you do. (In the case of corporate purchasing departments, I guess their compromise is that they're buying from you instead of from someone else.) And all the while, they put the happy face on their negotiations.[3]

Win-win in this sense follows the old Soviet approach to "getting to yes" in its negotiations with the West during the Cold War era: "What's ours is ours; what's yours is negotiable."

As Gordon told readers of *Harvard Management Communication Letter,* "If you read the classic texts, they talk about extreme opening positions, getting the other side to make a concession first, offering to split the difference only after both sides have gone a few rounds, and so on." In Gordon's view, concessions are not necessary. "Instead, you look for creative options . . . If there is a range of possible acceptable outcomes, then there is always a set of outcomes that will make both of us happier than the minimum acceptable outcome would."[2]

CREATIVE OPTIONS

The Negotiator's Dilemma: A Preview

Few business negotiations are purely distributive or purely integrative. Most are integrative to some degree, containing opportunities for both competition and collaboration. Indeed, the playing field of negotiations is better described as a continuum that includes those two extremes and mixtures of the two in between. Knowing where to play in that continuum involves a tension known as the negotiator's dilemma. "Should I compete for as big a share of this small pie as possible," one participant asks, "but risk having the other side claim the value? Or should I collaborate in hopes of doing well?" These questions involve difficult strategic choices, which means balancing competitive strategies with cooperative strategies. Knowing whether to compete where interests conflict—claiming more instead of less—or to create value by exchanging the information that leads to mutually advantageous options is at the core of the negotiator's art.

The negotiator's dilemma is explored at greater length in chapter 6.

Fisher, Ury, and Patton's popular book *Getting to Yes* supports this view. It shifted people's focus from I-win-you-lose situations to integrative negotiations, in which each party can claim satisfaction. Some have mistaken this to mean that everybody can get everything they want (win-win), which is not what the authors meant. They provide approaches both for creating value (focus on interests, not position; separate the people from the problem) and for "principled" value claiming (identify objective standards). Likewise, other authors, notably David Lax and James Sebenius in *The Manager as Negotiator*, tell readers to focus on enlarging the pie through trades (creating value) while seeking to get a reasonable piece of the expanded pie for themselves (claiming value).

Finding opportunities for mutual benefit naturally requires information sharing. Unlike the distributive situation, in which you deliberately play your cards close to the vest, an integrative negotiation encourages negotiators to do the following:

- Provide significant information about their circumstances.

- Explain why they want to make a deal.

- Talk about their real interests or business constraints.

- Reveal and explain in general terms their preferences among issues or options.

- Consider and reveal any additional capabilities or resources they have that might meet the other side's interests and could be added to the deal.

- Use what they learn to find creative options that will meet the interests of both parties to the greatest extent possible.

Multiple Phases and Multiple Parties

When thinking about negotiating, most people envision one person or one team of people sitting across the table from another.[4] The individual parties eventually hammer out their differences or walk away. This characterization is often accurate. It describes how bosses and their direct reports deal with performance and pay issues, how an individual negotiates for the purchase of a new car, and so forth. Such negotiations are one-on-one and focus on a clear issue, and they are usually handled in a single meeting.

In reality, many negotiations are not so simple. They involve more than two parties, and they sometimes take place in phases, each devoted to one of several important issues. Though these more complex situations are beyond the scope of this book, you need to be aware of them. Each represents a "type" of negotiation.

Multiphase Negotiations

Multiphase transactions and the prospect of future dealings offer important advantages for parties who are trustworthy and who would like to foster cooperative behavior. In these situations, early phases allow the parties to build trust by performing their agreements as promised. A failure to perform warns the other side to be careful and to create enforcement mechanisms for agreements. Early phases also allow the parties to become familiar with each other's communication and negotiation styles. That familiarity often makes subsequent phases more productive.

Multiparty Negotiations

Business and professional negotiations commonly involve more than two parties, and certainly more than two people. Such *multiparty negotiations* can differ significantly from two-party negotiations in one important respect: Coalitions can form among the parties. Coalitions make it possible for weaker parties to gather the strength to push through their preferred proposals, or at least to block those they find unacceptable.

There are at least two types of coalitions: a *natural coalition* of allies who share a broad range of common interests, and a *single-issue coalition*, in which parties that differ on other issues unite to support or block a single issue (often for different reasons).

The challenge of multiparty negotiation is managing coalitions, breaking them apart or keeping them together depending on your own interests. Just as in a two-party negotiation, you must understand the goals, interests, and relationships of the many parties, and work from there.

A natural coalition of allies is hard to break. For example, an environmental agency and a citizen's nature conservation group share basic agendas and will often act in concert to block development initiatives, even without explicit agreement to do so.

A single-issue coalition of otherwise disassociated parties, in contrast, is generally more vulnerable. For example, a labor union and a nature conservation group might form a coalition to block an antiunion developer from building a shopping mall in a wooded area. Each has very different reasons for joining the blocking coalition, which makes it feasible for the other side to put a wedge between them. For example, if the property owner finds a different developer with a better track record in its dealing with unions, the union is likely to withdraw its opposition, leaving the conservationists to fight alone. Or, if the original developer agrees to move the project to a different location, the nature conservation group is likely to pull out, leaving the union as the sole opponent.

Summing Up

This chapter has introduced the basic types of negotiation you're likely to encounter, and what's at stake in each.

- A distributive negotiation pits two or more parties in competition for a fixed amount of value. Here, each side's goal is to claim as much value as possible, as in the sale of a rug at a street bazaar. Value gained by one party is unavailable to others.

- Integrative negotiation is about creating *and* claiming value. Through collaboration and information sharing, the parties look for opportunities to satisfy the key objectives of each, recognizing that they will probably have to give ground on other objectives.

- The negotiator's dilemma describes the situation faced by people who enter any type of bargaining situation. They must determine which game to play: aggressively claim the value currently on the table (and possibly come out the loser), or work with the other side to create even better opportunities that can be shared.

- No matter which type of negotiation you're faced with, it's bound to be more complex if it is multiphased or involves multiple parties. If your negotiation is multiphased, use the early phases to build trust and to become familiar with the other parties. If many parties are involved, consider the benefits of forming a coalition to improve your bargaining power.

Four Key Concepts

Your Starting Points

Key Topics Covered in This Chapter

- *BATNA (best alternative to a negotiated agreement)*

- *Reservation price*

- *ZOPA (zone of possible agreement)*

- *Value creation through trades*

WHEN PEOPLE don't have the power to force a desired outcome, they generally negotiate—but only when they believe it is to their advantage to do so. A negotiated solution is advantageous only under certain conditions, that is, when a better option is not available. Consider this example: One of your best employees, Charles, is being courted by another company. Replacing him will be costly, but perhaps not as costly as negotiating some combination of financial inducements and work changes that will persuade him to stay and keep on contributing. Your mental calculator tells you that the cost of these inducements is less painful than your only other option—losing a star employee.

Any successful negotiation must have a fundamental framework based on knowing the following:

- The alternative to negotiation

- The minimum threshold for a negotiated deal

- How flexible a party is willing to be, and what trade-offs it is willing to make

Three concepts are especially important for establishing this framework: BATNA (best alternative to a negotiated agreement), reservation price, and ZOPA (zone of possible agreement). This chapter develops these three concepts using distributed negotiations as examples. It then expands the framework to include a fourth concept: value creation through trade, switching to integrative negotiations for an example. This switch simultaneously illustrates how the concepts of reservation price and ZOPA shift when you move from distributive to integrative negotiations.

Know Your BATNA

BATNA, a concept developed by Roger Fisher and William Ury, is the acronym for best alternative to a negotiated agreement. It is one's preferred course of action in the absence of a deal. Knowing your BATNA means knowing what you will do or what will happen if you fail to reach agreement in the negotiation at hand. Consider this example:

> *A consultant is negotiating with a potential client about a month-long assignment. It's not clear what fee arrangement she'll be able to negotiate, or even if she'll reach an agreement. So before she meets with this potential client, she considers her best alternative to an acceptable agreement. In this case, the best alternative to a negotiated agreement—the consultant's BATNA—is spending that month developing marketing studies for other clients—work that she calculates can be billed out at $15,000.*

Always know your BATNA before entering into any negotiation. Otherwise, you won't know whether a deal makes sense or when to walk away. People who enter negotiations without this knowledge put themselves in a bad position. Being unclear about their BATNAs, some will reject a good offer that is much better than their alternatives because they are overly optimistic. For example, Fred has brought a damage suit against a former employer. That employer has offered to settle out of court for $80,000. But Fred wants more. "I know that I'm in the right and can get what I want if I don't settle, but go to court," he tells himself. Going to court is his best alternative to the $80,000 settlement offer. But how good is that alternative? Fred hasn't really done a thorough job of estimating the probability of winning in court, nor the size of a potential award. In other words, he has no real idea of the alternative to the employer's settlement offer.

A King Who Knew His BATNA

Long before the acronym BATNA was invented, savvy operators kept their best alternatives in mind as they dealt with opponents. Consider France's Louis XI, one of the most crafty monarchs in fifteenth-century Europe. When England's Edward IV brought his army across the Channel to grab territory from his weaker rival, the French king decided to negotiate. Knowing that his BATNA was to fight a long and costly war, Louis calculated that it was safer and cheaper to strike a deal with Edward. So he signed a peace treaty with the English in 1475, paying 50,000 crowns up front and an annuity of 50,000 crowns for the rest of Edward's life (which proved to be short). To seal the deal, Louis treated his royal counterpart and the English army to forty-eight hours of eating, drinking, and merrymaking. As an added token, he assigned the Cardinal of Bourbon to be Edward's "jolly companion" and to forgive his sins as he committed them.

As Edward and his army staggered back to their boats, ending the Hundred Years War, Louis remarked: "I have chased the English out of France more easily than my father ever did; he drove them out by force of arms while I have driven them out by force of meat pies and good wine." Such is the power of negotiating when you know your BATNA.

SOURCE: Richard Luecke, *Scuttle Your Ships Before Advancing* (New York: Oxford University Press, 1993), 49.

Others run the risk of accepting a weak offer, one that is less favorable than what they could have obtained elsewhere if there were no agreement ("I probably have some other options, but this seems like a good deal").

Strong and Weak BATNAs

Your best alternative to a negotiated agreement determines the point at which you can say no to an unfavorable proposal. If that BATNA is strong, you can negotiate for more favorable terms, knowing that you have something better to fall back on if a deal cannot be arranged. A weak BATNA, on the other hand, puts you in a weak bargaining position. Consider the position of the consultant in our earlier example if she had no other work lined up. In that case her alternative to a deal might be sitting around waiting for the phone to ring—a terrible position to be in during negotiations.

Whenever a negotiator has a weak BATNA (or hasn't taken the time to determine what that BATNA is), it is difficult to walk away from a proposal—no matter how paltry it might be. And if the other side knows that its opponent has a weak BATNA, the weak party has very little power to negotiate. Not that this stops some people from trying to drive a hard bargain. For example, in late 2001, an organized group of the unemployed in France threatened to strike if the government failed to meet their demand for higher unemployment benefits! Needless to say, this group had little negotiating power.

Take a minute to think about your own best alternative to whatever deal you are presently negotiating. Do you have one? Is it strong or weak? Can you quantify it?

Improving Your Position

A weak BATNA is not the end of the world. Whatever hand you've been dealt, here are three potential approaches to strengthening your position:

1. Improve your BATNA.

2. Identify the other side's BATNA.

3. Weaken the other party's BATNA.

Each of these options is discussed in the following sections.

IMPROVE YOUR BATNA BATNA seems a given. Our consultant has $15,000 of other work she can turn to if negotiations with the new client fail. But she might be able to expand that other work, thereby improving her BATNA and giving her a strong hand in negotiations. For instance, she might call her current client and say,

"You know those marketing studies you asked me to develop. For a slightly higher fee—say, $5,000 more—I could expand the scope of those studies to include sales estimates of your two leading competitors' products. Would you like me to do that?" If she got the go-ahead to expand the project, her new BATNA would be higher—$20,000.

Anything that can be done to improve your BATNA will strengthen your negotiating position. Take a minute to think of ways you could do that, given current circumstances.

If you have a strong BATNA—and if you are certain that it's much stronger than anything the other side can muster—don't be shy about it. Discreetly let the other side know that you're negotiating from a strong position.

IDENTIFY THE OTHER SIDE'S BATNA Knowledge of the other side's BATNA is another source of negotiation strength. Is its alternative to a deal strong or weak relative to yours? A good estimation of the other side's BATNA can be a big help to you. For instance, in the example given earlier, our consultant would have a stronger bargaining hand if she knew that her potential client would have to pay $25,000 to another firm for the same work. Twenty-five thousand dollars would be the client's BATNA; knowing that would help our consultant be more effective at the negotiating table. Better still, a little sleuthing might reveal that the competing consulting firms were booked solid for the next four months. If the work had to be done soon, the potential client would have a very weak BATNA, and our consultant could pursue negotiations with much greater confidence. "My price is $30,000, and I can begin the work later this month."

Thus, knowledge of the other side's BATNA is extremely helpful when you can obtain it. But how can you obtain that knowledge? The opposing negotiator won't tell you unless his BATNA is very strong. He may even bluff about it. Sometimes, however, the other party's circumstances can be discovered. Asking questions during the negotiation can help you learn about the other side's BATNA, but you can also learn in advance by doing the following:

- Contacting sources within the industry

- Checking potentially relevant business publications

A Caution on BATNA Values

Although it's absolutely essential that you know your own BATNA and try to estimate that of the other side, be aware that most people don't do a good job of estimating BATNA values. For example, Lax and Sebenius describe an experiment involving the value of a company up for sale. "Even given identical business information, balance sheets, income statements, and the like," they write, "those assigned to buy the company typically rate its true value as low, while those assigned to sell it give much higher best estimates. Neutral observers tend to rank the potential someplace in between."[1]

The lesson here is that BATNA values can be influenced by your personal perspective. So be as objective as possible. Check your thinking with a neutral third party.

- Reviewing annual reports (or public filings)

- Asking questions informally of the negotiator or others within the company

- Imagining what your interests, preferences, and needs would be if you were in their position

Knowing the other side's BATNA lets you know how far you can go. But other knowledge is equally important. For instance, the more you know about the other side's broader concerns, industry, corporate structure, and other deals and goals, the better able you will be to find creative ways of meeting their interests (preferably at low cost to you).

WEAKEN THE OTHER PARTY'S BATNA Anything that weakens the other side's alternative to a deal will improve your relative position. In some cases, weakening the other side's BATNA may be done directly.

*Final Haven, Inc., a Texas-based chain of funeral homes, had been ac-
quiring independently operated rivals in the northeastern United States
and was in preliminary negotiations with Jim and Barbara Stanley for
the purchase of their establishment in central Connecticut. When those
negotiations began, the Stanleys were confident that they could get a
high price since another funeral home operator in the area, Bob's Discount Funerals, had been saying for years that he'd like to buy them
out. "That's a fine funeral business you have there," he had told them
repeatedly. "If you ever want to sell it, talk to me." Bob had even
hinted at $800,000.*

*The Stanleys thought of $800,000 as their best alternative to cut-
ting a deal with Final Haven. "If we can play Bob off Final Haven,"
Jim Stanley told Barbara, "we should be able to get a still better
price—maybe $1 million." Needless to say, the Stanleys were crest-
fallen when the local newspaper announced "Bob's Discount Funerals
to Be Acquired by Texas-Based Chain." Their alternative had just
evaporated, leaving them in a weak position relative to the deal makers
from Final Haven.*

In this example, Final Haven neutralized Jim and Barbara's alternative deal. Their $800,000 BATNA had been taken off the table,
leaving continued operation of the business as their only alternative
to an offer by Final Haven. Thus, Final Haven strengthened its position relative to the other side by weakening the Stanleys' BATNA.
Of course, the Stanleys' position may not be entirely untenable. They

---

Determining Your BATNA

Would you like to identify your BATNA and explore ways of
improving it? Turn to the appendix to find a handy worksheet
whose questions take you through the steps. The worksheet and
other tools can also be found online at the Harvard Business Essentials Web site: www.elearning.hbsp.org/businesstools. This
site offers free interactive versions of the worksheets, checklists,
and other tools introduced in this series.

might take steps to strengthen their BATNA. For example, they might entice another potential bidder into the game—perhaps a rival chain of funeral homes.

When You Have No Alternatives

No negotiator is in a weaker position than one with no alternative to a deal. In this case, the other side can dictate the terms. The BATNA-less party is a deal *taker*, not a deal *maker*. If you find yourself in this dangerous situation, you must create an alternative. Writing in the *Harvard Business Review*, Danny Ertel described how Colbún, Chile's third-largest electric power producer, managed to do this:

> Colbún has often found itself at a substantial disadvantage in terms of scale and negotiating leverage. It had to bargain for transmission capacity, for example, with the transmission arm of the largest power company. If it had gone into those negotiations without an alternative, it would have been at the mercy of the other side, and it would have ended up paying dearly for the capacity. But Colbún had an express corporate policy requiring the establishment of a BATNA in any negotiation. Because there were no other existing options for purchasing transmission capacity, Colbún had to create one—developing its own transmission line, conducting feasibility studies, and even putting construction contracts out to bid.[2]

As described by Ertel, this approach worked. The other side steadily reduced its price quote as development of Colbún's BATNA progressed.

Are you without an alternative in any of your current negotiations—with your boss, with a customer, or with someone else? If you are, stop to think about how you could create one. Think, too, about which type of alternative would most strengthen your hand.

BATNA Is Not Always Simple

BATNA is a straightforward concept. But applying it is not as simple as we've made it appear. Most business negotiations involve many variables, some of which cannot be quantified or compared. This makes for a fuzzy BATNA. For example, let's suppose that you are contemplating the purchase of a used 2001 Volvo sedan with an automatic transmission and 28,000 miles on the odometer. The dealer has it listed for $26,000 and offers a ninety-day warranty. Your neighbor, however, owns a 2001 Volvo station wagon with a standard transmission (which you prefer) and 53,000 miles on the odometer. He says that it has no known mechanical problems, and will part with it for $18,000—with no warranty. As you negotiate with the car dealer, your neighbor's vehicle would seem to be your BATNA. But is it a useful benchmark of what you could achieve in the absence of an agreement?

If price were the only issue, the neighbor's Volvo would be your BATNA, but there are substantial quantitative and qualitative differences between the two vehicles. The neighbor's car has a lower price and a standard transmission—which you like—but it has higher mileage and no warranty—which you don't like. Most negotiations involve similar complexities.

In a transaction that involves price and various other features, such as the car example, you can make the BATNA less fuzzy by assigning a monetary value to the various features and adjusting the BATNA value by that amount. For example, you could assign a price penalty of $4,000 to your neighbor's Volvo to adjust for its higher mileage, and another $1,000 for the fact that it comes with no warranty. At the same time, you could add a price premium of $500 to that same car for the fact that it has the standard transmission, which you prefer. Netting these adjustments, you have $4,500 (or $4,000 + $1,000 − $500). Add these to the neighbor's offer of $18,000 and you have $22,500—your new, less fuzzy BATNA. If the auto dealer would reduce his asking price to $22,500, you'd be indifferent as to which car you'd buy—at least theoretically.

Not all situations are amenable to price adjustments, for the simple reason that price is not always the fulcrum of negotiated deals. Qualitative issues also matter. For example, a person who is negotiating the purchase of a small business may be concerned with *when* the transaction will take place and with the *level* of the current owner's involvement as a consultant. In these cases, the negotiator must be able to make trade-offs in both sizing up the deal and developing his or her BATNA.

Reservation Price

The *reservation price* (also referred to as the *walk-away*) is the least favorable point at which one will accept a deal. Your reservation price should be derived from your BATNA, but it is not usually the same thing. If the deal is only about money, however, and a credible dollar offer is your BATNA, then your reservation price would be approximately equal to your BATNA.

Consider the following example:

> You are currently paying $20 per square foot for suburban office space. The location is satisfactory and you believe that the price is fair, but you wouldn't mind paying more to be closer to your downtown customers. While preparing to negotiate with a commercial landlord for an office lease in a downtown high-rise, you decided that you would not pay more than $30 per square foot. That's your reservation price. If the landlord insists on more, you can walk away and attempt to lease space in a different building. Or you can stay where you are at $20 per square foot (your BATNA).
>
> At the end of a lengthy negotiation session, the landlord declares that he will not accept less than $35 per square foot—and he won't budge. You graciously terminate the negotiation and walk away from the deal.

In this example your reservation price is different from your BATNA. BATNA in this case is the current rent at the current location: $20 per square foot. But the new location has different characteristics

---

Setting Your Reservation Price

Do you know your reservation price in your current negotiations? What variables affect your price? What value have you traded off in figuring your walk-away? The appendix contains a handy worksheet that can help you set an objective reservation price. The worksheet and other tools can also be found online at the Harvard Business Essentials Web site: www.elearning.hbsp. org/businesstools. The site offers free interactive versions of the worksheets, checklists, and other tools introduced in this series.

that enter into the equation. It's closer to customers, and it may be a more attractive space with greater workplace utility. You'd be willing to assume the added expense and the hassle of moving, even if it meant paying $30 per square foot. Anything more than that, however, would be unacceptable. Thus, there's a subtle difference between your BATNA and your reservation price.

The fact that the prospective landlord would not take less than $35 per square foot suggests that $35 is his reservation price.

ZOPA

The *ZOPA*, or zone of possible agreement, is a third key concept to remember. ZOPA is the area or range in which a deal that satisfies both parties can take place. Put another way, it is the set of agreements that potentially satisfy both parties.

Each party's reservation price determines one end of the ZOPA. The ZOPA itself exists (if at all) in the overlap between these high and low limits, that is, between the parties' reservation prices. Consider this example:

> *A buyer has set a reservation price of $275,000 for the purchase of a commercial warehouse. "That's as high as I'm willing to go," she tells herself. Naturally, she would prefer paying less. Unbeknownst to her, the seller has set a reservation price of $250,000. That is the least he'll take for the property. The ZOPA, therefore, is the range between $250,000 and $275,000, as shown in figure 2-1. The two parties might haggle a bit in reaching agreement, but an agreement in this range would satisfy each.*

FIGURE 2-1

Zone of Possible Agreement

BUYER: "What would you say to an offer of $255,000? I could agree to that."

SELLER: "Thanks, but I believe that the building is worth more—and I can get more if I leave the building on the market for another month or so."

BUYER: "Maybe, but maybe not. I'd be willing to pay $260,000 now if we could reach an agreement."

SELLER: "$265,000 and it's yours."

BUYER: "Then $265,000 it is."

In this commonplace example, each party had a reservation price, and they bargained within the ZOPA. In doing so, each got a better price than his or her walk-away. We can assume here that neither knew the reservation price of his or her counterpart. As you can imagine, that knowledge would have been extremely valuable. For example, with foreknowledge of the other side's reservation price, the buyer might have driven a tougher bargain, holding out for something closer to $250,000. Estimating the other side's reservation price is sometimes possible. If, for example, equivalent properties in the area were listed for $260,000, the buyer could assume with some confidence that the seller's reservation price would be close to that figure. Likewise, if investigation revealed that the seller was highly motivated to sell, the buyer would offer less.

Now consider what would happen if the numbers were reversed—that is, if the buyer had set a reservation price of $250,000 and the seller had set a reservation price of $275,000. That is, the buyer won't pay more than $250,000, and the seller wouldn't take anything less than $275,000. There would be no overlap in the ranges in which the two parties could reach agreement—no ZOPA. No agreement would be possible, no matter how skilled the negotiators, unless there were other elements of value to be considered or if one or both sides' reservation prices changed. For example, if the warehouse seller determined that the potential buyer needed parking space for ten delivery trucks, and if he happened to have that many unused spaces available at an adjacent location, he might offer them to the seller as part of the package. That "sweetener" might break the impasse. This would be an example of the way value is created in integrative negotiations, as described in chapter 1. Information sharing makes it possible.

Value Creation Through Trades

Another fundamental concept of negotiation is value creation through trades. This concept tells us that negotiating parties can improve their positions by trading the values at their disposal. Value creation through trades occurs in the context of integrated negotiations. It usually takes the form of each party getting something it wants in return for something it values much less. Consider the following example:

> Helen and John are collectors of rare books and view their holdings as sources of artistic satisfaction and investment gain. "With rare books I can achieve a higher financial return than I can in the stock market," says Helen confidently, "and I experience the exquisite pleasure of having these wonderful first editions in my home." Helen's pride and joy is her set of Hemingway novels. She has every one in a first printing, with the exception of For Whom the Bell Tolls. She is negotiating with John, who has a copy for sale.
>
> John is pleased to have his original Hemingway, but as negotiations over the phone reveal, his primary interest is in building a collection of the works of the nineteenth-century American historian William Prescott. He currently has first printings of Prescott's multivolume History of the Reign of Ferdinand and Isabella and is aggressively looking for Volume 2 of that same author's The Conquest of Mexico. As luck would have it, Helen has a first printing of Volume 2, and is agreeable to parting with it since it is not part of any collection she is building. It is merely something she had purchased at an estate sale.
>
> In the end, John sells Helen the Hemingway book, completing her set, for $100 plus her copy of Prescott's Volume 2, which completes his set.
>
> Both are extremely happy with the deal.

This is a case in which two individuals were able to create value, not simply claim it. Both emerged with substantial satisfaction from the deal. This was possible because the goods exchanged had only modest value to their original holders, but exceptional value to their new owners.

Think for a moment about your own negotiations—with customers, suppliers, and fellow employees. Are you pulling and tugging with each other in a win-lose framework? Now think of ways that you might be able to satisfy the other side with something that would cost you very little.

- For a supplier, that greater value might take the form of an extended delivery period. For the customer, having deliveries spread out during the month might be of no great consequence, but for a supplier with strained production facilities, it may be very important.

- For a customer, greater value at low cost might take the form of three months of free repair services if needed. For a vendor who has great confidence that its products will need no repairs during that period, free service is nothing of consequence. In providing it to the customer the vendor incurs little cost, even though the customer values the repair service highly.

- For another department in your company, greater value might be found in your offer of two high-powered workstations that your people rarely if ever use. That department may be able to offer something in exchange that you value more than it does.

- For an employee, the opportunity to work from a home office two days each week may produce great satisfaction while costing the employer nothing.

Few of the things that others value highly will have little value to you, and vice versa. But they are sometimes there, and a little thinking and probing can identify them. That's value creation. Just be sure that if you give something of value, then you ask for something in trade.

Summing Up

This chapter has explained the fundamental concepts used by skilled negotiators.

- BATNA is the best alternative to a negotiated agreement. It is one's preferred course of action in the absence of a deal. Knowing your BATNA means knowing what you will do or what will happen if you fail to reach agreement. Don't enter a negotiation without knowing your BATNA.

- If your BATNA is weak, do what you can to improve it. Anything that strengthens your BATNA improves your negotiating position.

- Identify the other side's BATNA. If it is strong, think of what you can do to weaken it.

- Reservation price is the price at which the rational negotiator will walk away. Don't enter a negotiation without a clear reservation price.

- ZOPA is the zone of possible agreement. It is the area in which a deal will satisfy all parties. This area exists when the parties have different reservation prices, as when a home buyer is willing to pay up to $275,000 and the home seller is willing to take an offer that is at least $250,000.

- Value creation through trades is possible when a party has something he or she values less than does the other party— and vice versa. By trading these values, the parties lose little but gain greatly.

3

Preparation

Nine Steps to a Deal

Key Topics Covered in This Chapter

- *Understanding your own and the other side's interests and BATNA*

- *Identifying potential opportunities for value creation*

- *Determining the authority levels of both sides in a negotiation*

- *Understanding the people and the culture of the other side*

- *Preparing for flexibility*

- *Showing the fairness of one's position*

- *Altering the process in your favor*

EVERY IMPORTANT ENDEAVOR benefits from preparation. Negotiating is no different. People who know
what they want, what they are willing to settle for, and
what the other side is all about stand a better chance of negotiating
a favorable deal for themselves, as the following example makes clear.

*Laura, one of Phil's best employees, requested a meeting to talk about
taking a six-month leave of absence. She had expressed her interest in
an extended leave several times over the past several months. But now
she made a formal request for a meeting. "Let's meet a week from Tues-
day at 4 o'clock to discuss it," said Phil.*

    *With all the things going on in the department, Phil didn't want
to think about how his unit would get its work done without Laura.
And so he didn't think about her request. "Maybe she'll change her
mind or just forget about it," he mused. But she didn't.*

    *When they finally met, Laura was completely prepared. She had
picked potential starting and ending dates for her leave. She'd checked
with the human resource department about leave policies and the staffing
issues. And she anticipated the issues her boss would raise: Who will pick
up the slack? How will deadlines be met? Who will take her place in
team activities? Laura had prepared answers for each of these questions.*

    *Phil, on the other hand, was winging it. He didn't like the idea of
extended leaves. "What if everybody decided to do this?" he muttered.
"We'd have chaos around here." But whenever he raised an objection,
Laura came back with an effective response. He wanted to suggest an
alternative to such a long leave, but couldn't think of one.*

In the end, Laura got her leave on her terms because she was pre-
pared and Phil was not. Had he been prepared, Phil might have found
common ground on which his unit goals and Laura's goals could have
been mutually satisfied.

For the negotiator, preparation means understanding one's own position and interests, the position and interests of the other party or parties, the issues at stake, and alternative solutions. It means learning as much as possible about concepts introduced in the previous chapter: your BATNA and reservation price and those of the other parties, the zone within which an agreement can be struck, and opportunities to create more value. It also means understanding the people with whom you'll be dealing. We'll explore these and other preparation issues through nine steps.[1]

Step 1: Consider What a Good Outcome Would Be for You and the Other Side

Never enter into a negotiation without first asking yourself, "What would be a good outcome for me? What are my needs, and how do I prioritize them?" Then ask the same questions from the perspective of the other side.

In the example that introduced this chapter, Phil, the manager, should have thought ahead to the outcomes that would have been good for him—outcomes that would allow his unit to reach its assigned goals. The most obvious would be for Laura to stay put. But that isn't feasible, since the company has a leave policy. And turning her request down flat might lead to her resignation, creating a still bigger problem. But that's the extreme outcome. There are plenty of others that might allow Phil's unit to get its work done. For example:

- Negotiate a shorter leave.

- Schedule the leave for the slow part of the year.

- Ask Laura to work out a plan with her coworkers that clearly accommodates the business needs of the unit.

Any of these outcomes might satisfy Phil.

But what about Laura's perspective? If she has any bargaining power, her concept of a good outcome will limit Phil's ability to produce the best outcome for himself. So as part of his preparation, Phil needs to put himself in her shoes and ask the same questions: "What would be a good outcome for Laura? What are her needs, and how does she prioritize them?" Logically, Phil can only answer these questions if he understands Laura and her motive in seeking a leave of absence in the first place.

Since Phil hasn't bothered to understand Laura's issues, let's play mind reader and find out what she's thinking.

> *I really need to spend more time with my son Nathan. He's a very unfocused teenager. And it shows in his school reports. He's not doing his homework, he's goofing off in class, and his grades are lousy. Someone needs to get him on track or he'll never get into a decent college or develop good work habits. Someone should be there when he gets home from school to enforce study habits and to provide a family dinner during which we listen to each other. His father can't do it—he travels too much. And I can't do it with a full-time job. I don't get home until 6:30, and by then I'm pooped! That long commute is just killing me.*
>
> *I need some time off to get that boy on track. Six months might do it. We really can't afford the lost income, but we can't let our son continue to drift either.*

Had Phil prepared himself by learning why Laura wanted a leave, he would have been able to postulate one or more good outcomes from her perspective.

Negotiating experts refer to the interests of the various parties when they urge people to prepare. Without understanding those interests—one's own and those of the other parties—a good outcome is generally elusive. Determining the interests of the other side, however, is sometimes difficult, especially when that side conceals its interests, as in the example of an independent sales representative who is negotiating with a manufacturer for the exclusive right to distribute its equipment in one particular region of the country. Negotiators for the manufacturer are tight-lipped about their long-term interests vis-à-vis this sales rep because they want to eventually replace him with one of their own people.

The interests of the two sides are sometimes revealed through dialogue at the negotiating table. But not always—particularly in win-lose distributive deals. If you cannot identify the other side's interests, use every communication opportunity to probe for them. Or try using the checklist "Assessing the Other Side's Position and Interests" found in the appendix. (The worksheet and other tools can also be found online at the Harvard Business Essentials Web site: www.elearning.hbsp.org/businesstools.)

Step 2: Identify Potential
Value Creation Opportunities

Once you understand what a good outcome would look like from your vantage point and from the vantage point of the other side, you can then identify areas of common ground, compromise, and opportunities for favorable trades. If Phil eventually recognized Laura's key issue as one of balance between work and family life, for instance, he could prepare himself with a handful of feasible alternatives that would allow both parties to attain most, if not all, of their goals. For example:

- Reduced hours for Laura—9 A.M. to 2 P.M. Laura would be home in time to deal with her son, and Phil could use her salary reduction to hire a temp to fill the 2-to-5 P.M. time gap.

- Telework from a home office from 8 A.M. to 3:30 P.M. This would address Laura's interests with respect to her long commute, her desire to provide closer supervision for her son in the late afternoon, *and* her concern about losing significant income. Laura could, in turn, address Phil's interests by developing a plan for timely delivery of all her work.

Laura might see either of these alternatives as superior to her initial leave request in that each would have her at home in the early afternoon and still provide her with most—if not all—of her income. And neither would create serious problems for Phil's unit. In this sense the negotiation would be value creating. Laura would get the time she needed for work/life balance, and Phil would retain a good employee and keep his department running on an even keel.

Any time value is created, you need to answer the question of who will claim that value. One party could claim 100 percent of it, or it could be shared in some way. Naturally, if you help create value through negotiation, you'll want to claim a share—you'd be entitled to it. This is what sellers do in negotiated business acquisitions.

> *Wholesome Products, Inc., is being purchased by Conglomerated Foods in a friendly takeover. Although Wholesome's shares trade for $50 per share on the stock exchange, Conglomerated is willing to pay $65 per share. Why? Among other reasons, the acquirer sees valuable synergies in putting the two companies together. That extra value did not exist in Wholesome as a stand-alone company, and it might not exist if some other company were making the acquisition. But as Conglomerated sees it, adding Wholesome to its portfolio is equivalent to making two plus two equal five.*

In settling on a premium for the share price, both companies in this example are claiming their newly created value: Wholesome shareholders get more money and, even at that price, Conglomerated's management thinks it has scored a good deal because of its anticipated synergies.

Step 3: Identify your BATNA and Reservation Price, and Do the Same for the Other Side

The previous chapter discussed BATNA and reservation price at length. We mention these concepts again here because they are such important elements of preparation.

Getting back to the example of Phil and Laura, what is Phil's BATNA? The story hasn't given us enough details to know for certain, but it appears that Phil hasn't even thought about his BATNA. He doesn't have anyone waiting in the wings to replace Laura if he says "no" and she resigns. If he walks away from negotiating her leave request, he'll be faced with either (1) dealing with a disgruntled employee if she stays, or (2) hiring a replacement if she leaves. Neither is a pleasant prospect from Phil's viewpoint. If Laura surmises this as part of her preparation, she'll be in a better position to negotiate.

Laura's BATNA is also limited. If she doesn't negotiate with Phil, she'll more than likely get her leave since company policy provides for it. But saying, "Give me a leave or I'll sue" would undermine her standing in the company—something she doesn't want. So her best alternative to a negotiated deal may be resigning and looking for a new job six months down the road. If Phil understands this, he will be better prepared to bargain.

Step 4: Shore Up Your BATNA

(Support)

As described in the previous chapter, anything you can do to improve your best alternative to a negotiated deal will put you in a stronger position. In the case of Phil and Laura, Phil could have improved his BATNA in the preparation stage if he had identified another

---

How Needy Are You?

Author and consultant Jim Camp urges his readers to avoid appearing "needy," the equivalent of having a weak BATNA. Shrewd bargainers will take advantage of that neediness. If opponents don't have it, tough negotiators will do whatever they can to encourage neediness in their opponents:

intelligent / tactical (accurate)

> *Tough negotiators are experts at recognizing this neediness in their adversaries, and expert in creating it as well. Negotiators with giant corporations, in particular, will heighten the expectations of their supplier adversaries, painting rosy, exaggerated scenarios for mega-orders, joint ventures, global alliances, all for the purposes of building neediness on the part of their adversary. . . . Then, when the neediness is well-established, they lower the boom with changes, exceptions, and . . . demands for concessions.[2]*

You can avoid appearing needy by building a strong BATNA—and letting the other side know that you are prepared to walk away if it demands too many concessions.

employee willing and able to step into Laura's shoes if she drove too hard a bargain. Laura's strongest bargaining chip is her importance to the smooth working of the unit. If she could be rendered "replaceable," that chip would lose its power.

Shoring up one's BATNA is an important part of preparation, but is not limited to the "pre-negotiations" phase. Good negotiators work to improve their BATNAs before *and* during deliberations with the other side.

Step 5: Anticipate the Authority Issue

Conventional wisdom insists that the negotiator on the other side of the table must have full authority. Otherwise, you risk falling victim to the old "car dealer" trick, where just as you are about to reach agreement with the salesman, he says, "I'll have to clear this with my manager." In other words, the negotiation with the salesman is used to bring you to your bottom line; the second negotiation, with the manager, aims to push you beyond it.

There are real advantages to negotiating with the person who has the power to sign on the dotted line:

- All of your reasoning is heard directly by the decision maker.

- The benefits of the good relationship built at the bargaining table are likely to be reflected in the deal and its implementation.

- There are fewer chances of disputes or misinterpretation of particular provisions.

- You avoid the "car dealer" trick described previously.

- If your aim is to make the person on the other side of the table hungry for a deal with you, your efforts will do no good if the real decision maker is somewhere in the background.

So do whatever you can to identify the real decision maker. Don't be afraid to ask, "Who will make the decision?" If that person is not on the negotiating team, suggest that he or she be included. "If

Mr. Jones will be making the decision, wouldn't it be best if he participate with us? That way we can avoid misunderstandings and save time." If your decision maker is at the table, press the other side to reciprocate.

Also try to find out *how* the other side will make its decision. Is it up to one individual, a team, or a committee? Will the decision be kicked around the organization for a week or two? Don't be shy about asking point-blank, "What decision-making process do you use for an issue like this one?"

As a practical matter, you won't always be able to negotiate with the individual (or committee) who retains final authority. Even deals negotiated by the president of the United States—arguably the most powerful individual in the nation—must be ratified by the U.S. Senate.

Dealing with negotiators who lack full authority, however, may have advantages: These individuals may be freer to discuss their company's interests and to explore creative options. If you are dealing with someone who does not have full authority, view this as freedom from the need to commit. But observe these cautions:

- Confirm the ground rule that neither side will be committing his or her company in the negotiation. (If they're not committing, you shouldn't have to either.)

- Suggest using the opportunity to discuss your respective interests and to come up with creative options and packages.

- When negotiating about dollar issues, leave yourself some *wiggle room* in case the final negotiator pushes harder in a second round. If there's no wiggle room, strongly convey the message that this is your best offer.

Instead of insisting that the person on the other side of the bargaining table has full authority, it's more important that you determine the *authority level* of the person with whom you will be negotiating, so that you can plan accordingly. Thus, try to ascertain the following:

- Who will be at the negotiating table

- What is that person's title and area of responsibility

- How long the other side's representative has been with the company

- How the company is structured (Is it very hierarchical, with significant decision-making powers centered at the top, or is it relatively decentralized?)

- How the negotiator is viewed within the organization (Is he or she generally respected and listened to, or not?)

Understand the role of negotiator

Granted, this information may be difficult to obtain, but it's well worth digging for. If you know other players in the industry or business community, you may be able to learn this through an informal, off-the-record phone call or two.

If you learn that the negotiator for the other side has very little formal authority and is not respected or listened to by the decision makers, you have a problem. Working with this person may simply waste your time. So try to get another representative to participate in the negotiations. One tactful way to do this is to suggest that you will be bringing a colleague (either with more formal authority or because your joint recommendation will carry more weight), and request that the other side do the same.

As for your side, always know exactly how much authority you have in a negotiation. For example:

- Are you authorized only to commit to a predetermined range of deals for which committee approval has been obtained? What if you can negotiate something better? What would the committee consider to be better?

- Are you authorized to commit to a deal that meets certain financial objectives, with freedom to structure the deal in the best way you can? Would your company prefer that you bring such a deal back for formal review and approval?

- Is your authority limited on dollar issues but not on other creative options without significant financial implications?

- Are you authorized to provide information about your company's needs, interests, and preferences if the other side engages in a good-faith, reciprocal exchange?

You may be frustrated if you don't get the authority you seek, but at least you won't unwittingly overstep your bounds. Here again, less authority is sometimes better. The need to check back for certain decisions may be strategically helpful, and may enable you to be more creative in inventing options.

Step 6: Learn All You Can About the Other Side's People and Culture, Their Goals, and How They've Framed the Issue

Negotiating is, at bottom, an interpersonal activity. Seasoned negotiators understand this and make a point of learning as much as they can about the people with whom they must deal. Who are those individuals on the other side of the table? Are they experienced negotiators or novices? Are they aggressive or are they conflict-avoiding accommodators? Is the culture of their organization bureaucratic or entrepreneurial? Are the people at the table authorized to make a deal, or must they run back to their bosses for instructions and approval? Perhaps more important, what are they attempting to achieve and how critical is this negotiation to their business? Seeking answers to these questions is part of pre-negotiation preparation and should continue at the table itself. You should, for example, ask the other side to provide the names and titles of its negotiating team. Once you have those names, ask around your company or around the industry, "What can anyone tell me about these individuals? Has anyone dealt with them before?" Their titles may help answer the question of whether they are authorized to make a deal.

Step 7: Prepare for Flexibility in the Process— Don't Lock Yourself into a Rigid Sequence

Negotiations don't always follow a predictable or linear path. Relationships sometimes sour. Unanticipated developments cause one side to withdraw or freeze talks. Newly found opportunities encourage the other side to drive a harder bargain. One negotiator is replaced by another. These developments mean that the parties must be prepared to move forward without a clear roadmap. They must also exercise patience, because many negotiations have on-again off-again qualities. Managers who have earned their spurs in operations—where "let's get it done now" is the watchword—are not naturally disposed to patience. But it is a virtue they need in negotiating.

Here are some things you can do to be more flexible in negotiations:

- Start with the assumption that the process will not unfold in a predictable, linear fashion.

- Be prepared for changes on both sides: new people and unanticipated developments.

- Treat every change as an opportunity for learning.

Flexibility is important, but be flexible within the context of your larger goal. If, for example, your goal in a negotiation is to acquire a particular business, keep that goal uppermost in your mind. Alter the pace as needed. Be patient when unanticipated delays occur. But never allow these bumps in the road to make you lose sight of your goal.

Step 8: Gather External Standards and Criteria Relevant to Fairness

Both sides want to believe that any deal reached is fair and reasonable. And if the parties expect to have a continuing relationship, a sense of fairness and reasonableness matters. Neither party should feel that it has been forced to make a bad deal.

External or "objective" criteria can often be used to establish what is fair and reasonable. For example, you might be able to say something like this:

> I've spent some time researching the commission structures used by commercial real estate agencies in the metropolitan area. As you can see, for properties listed between $1 million and $3 million, the commission rates range between 3 percent and 5 percent, with an average of 4.4 percent. Thus, we believe that our offer to pay you a 4.5 percent commission is both fair and reasonable.

Because there are often many relevant criteria for fairness and reasonableness, an important part of preparation is (1) researching which criteria might be applied, (2) being prepared to show why those more favorable to you are more relevant, and (3) being prepared to show why those less favorable to you are less relevant. If you can convince the other side that a certain criterion or formula is fair and reasonable, they will find it harder to reject a proposal incorporating that standard, and they are more likely to feel satisfied with the deal.

Step 9: Alter the Process in Your Favor

Have you ever felt that your ideas were being ignored during meetings or formal negotiations? Does it ever appear that these meetings are rigged to produce a particular result—in spite of input by you or others? If you have, consider these possible explanations:

- Whoever set the agenda did so with a particular outcome in mind—one that benefits that person or entity.

- People are deferring to someone with greater organizational clout—your arguments notwithstanding.

- Yours is a "lone voice in the wilderness" and out of step with others.

Any of these explanations can shut you out and steer results in a direction favored—if not rigged—by someone else. The antidote is to work away from the table to change the process. "Process moves," as described by Deborah Kolb and Judith Williams, "do not address the substantive issues in a negotiation." Instead, they directly affect the hearing those issues receive. "The agenda, the pre-negotiation groundwork, and the sequence in which ideas and people are heard— all these structural elements influence others' receptivity to opinions and demands."[3]

If you've ever followed international conflict negotiations on the evening news, you've probably noticed that experienced diplomats don't jump right into the issues. Instead, they spend months trying to agree where the meeting will take place, who will participate, and even the shape of the negotiating table. These are all process moves, and effective preparation includes attention to these away-from-the-table issues. Kolb and Williams make these specific recommendations about process moves:

- **Work behind the scenes to educate others on your ideas.** A formal meeting is not always a good venue for making a detailed case, or for holding dialogue about a complex issue—especially when opponents control the agenda. So educate other participants one on one outside formal meetings. Concentrate on people who are respected centers of influence. Convince these people that your ideas have merit, and they will back you when opponents try to ignore your position during meetings. Better still, form a coalition of support outside the negotiations.

- **Reframe the process.** If you're been marginalized in a series of meetings or negotiations, the process may be the reason. Consider this example: A loud and brash department head has framed an upcoming meeting in terms of her need for more resources—resources that will have to come from your department. She's prepared to wrestle for as much as she can get, confident that others at the meeting will be neutral because they will not be affected. You could counter by reframing the discussion from "her needs" to "the company's needs." This would make you appear levelheaded and statesmanlike, and would help others recognize that the department head's resource grab also affects them.

We'll have more on framing in the next chapter.

As you prepare for a negotiation, recognize that you'll never learn as much as you'd like. Learning about the issues and about the other side is always limited by time, the cost of gathering information, and the fact that some information will be deliberately hidden. So be prepared to learn as negotiations unfold.

Summing Up

If your aim is to be an effective negotiator, take the time and make the effort needed to become fully prepared. This chapter has offered nine preparatory steps:

1. Know what a good outcome would be from your point of view and that of the other side.

2. Look for opportunities to create value in the deal.

3. Know your BATNA and reservation price. Make an effort to estimate those benchmarks for the other side.

4. If your BATNA isn't strong, find ways to improve it.

5. Find out if the person or team you're dealing with has the authority to make a deal.

6. Know those with whom you're dealing. Learn as much as you can about the people and the culture on the other side and how they've framed the issue.

7. If a future relationship with the other side matters, gather the external standards and criteria that will show your offer to be fair and reasonable.

8. Don't expect things to follow a linear path to a conclusion. Be prepared for bumps in the road and periodic delays.

9. Alter the agenda and process moves in your favor.

Table Tactics

How to Play the Game Well

Key Topics Covered in This Chapter

- *Getting the other side to the table*

- *Getting off to a good start*

- *Harnessing the power of anchoring*

- *Using concessionary moves*

- *Tactics for integrative (win-win) negotiations: active listening, exploiting complementary interests, and packaging options for more favorable deals*

- *General tactics: framing and continual evaluation*

MOST NEWCOMERS enter into negotiations with substantial concerns. Should they be tough or collaborative? Should they hold firm to their price or be prepared to make concessions? Is it best to fight hard for the most they can get or seek a fair outcome? Should they make the first offer or wait to counter it? This chapter addresses these and other tactical questions for both integrative and distributive negotiations.[1] It begins with tactics you can use to get the ball rolling—that is, to get the other side to negotiate.

Getting the Other Side to the Table

Before we get into actual negotiating *tactics,* let's consider some tactics for getting the other side to negotiate. In many cases, issues you may want to negotiate cannot move forward because one or more parties simply aren't interested—they are satisfied with the status quo. They see no point in negotiating with you. And if they have greater organizational power than you, they may brush you off with these types of comments: "I don't think there is any reason to consider this—things are fine," or "We're so tied up with the budget that I won't be able to consider that until next spring at the earliest."

Writing in the *Harvard Business Review,* Deborah Kolb and Judith Williams note: "Such resistance is a natural part of the informal negotiation process. A concern will generally be accorded a fair hearing only when someone believes two things: the other party has something desirable, and one's own objectives will not be met without giving something in return. Willingness to negotiate is, therefore, a confession of mutual need."

More precisely, resisters must conclude that they will be better off if they negotiate and worse off if they do not. Kolb and Williams suggest three things you can do to help reluctant bargainers reach this conclusion:

1. **Offer incentives.** What are the reluctant person's needs: money, time, your support? Determine those needs and then pose them as potential benefits of negotiations. For example, if your boss, the sales manager, is reluctant to give you time to work on a redesign of the company's inventory system, explain how an improved system will help solve one of his problems—lost sales from out-of-stock conditions.

2. **Put a price on the status quo.** Spell out the cost of not negotiating. Kolb and Williams use the example of a woman whose boss promoted her and had her take on additional work, but was forever delaying any discussion of a pay raise. Frustrated by his inaction, she found a way to get his attention—she secured a job offer from another company. The boss was suddenly very interested in dealing with her long overdue pay raise. He had to negotiate or face the costly and time-consuming process of replacing an effective subordinate. In other words, he realized the price of the status quo.

3. **Enlist support.** Allies can sometimes accomplish what other measures cannot. For example, if the sales manager described earlier still will not give you time off to improve the inventory system, look for allies who have organizational power *and* a reason to favor your goal. The chief financial officer, for instance, will likely favor any plan to improve inventory management. The CFO knows that better inventory management means lower working capital requirements, which makes her look good. Once the sales manager realizes that the issue has risen to the senior management level, he's likely to bargain.

Use one or more of these tactics, and the other party will see the virtue of negotiating with you.

Making a Good Start

Once you've gotten the other side to the bargaining table, it's important to get things off to a smooth start. That begins with relieving the tension that is often present. In your opening remarks, try to relieve that tension:

- Express respect for the other side's experience and expertise.

- Frame the task positively, as a joint endeavor.

- Emphasize your openness to the other side's interests and concerns.

Tips for Establishing the Right Tone

The negotiating environment can affect the level of tension and openness that prevails. If you're interested in lowering tension and seeking collaborative discussion, follow these tips:

- Never underestimate the value of "breaking bread." In practically every culture, breaking bread is a bonding ritual. So have coffee, soft drinks, and light snacks available.

- Use small talk at the beginning to dispel tension, lower people's natural defenses, and begin the process of building relationships. Even in a win-lose negotiation, small talk helps the different sides know each other better and gauge each other's truthfulness. It may also loosen people up to the point of seeking value-creating opportunities.

- Learn from what the small talk reveals about the other negotiator's style and manner.

- If the other side is very formal, don't speak too casually—they may interpret this as a lack of seriousness on your part. If the other side is decidedly informal, speak in a more casual way, perhaps using metaphors with which they are comfortable.

After these opening remarks, start with the agenda, making sure both parties have a common understanding of the issues to be covered. Then, explicitly discuss the process, especially since people often hold different assumptions about how the negotiation should work. Some assume that there will be haggling. Some expect proposals to be made at the outset, while others expect an open discussion of the issues to come first. Listen carefully to the discussion of process—it will tell you a great deal about the other side's negotiating style. Offer to explain some of your interests and concerns first. This is a good-faith demonstration that you are prepared to disclose information, provided that the exchange is reciprocal. If the other side does not reciprocate with information, be very cautious about providing more information.

Tactics for Win–Lose Negotiations

In some negotiations, every gain by one side represents a loss to the other. Chapter 1 defined these as distributive negotiations. Not all negotiations pit one party directly against the other, but many do. The tactics described in this section will help you be more successful in these situations.

Anchoring

Anchoring is an attempt to establish a reference point around which negotiations will make adjustments. In some cases, you can gain an advantage by putting the first offer on the table. That first offer can become a strong psychological anchor: It becomes the reference point of subsequent pulling and pushing by the participants. As described by Max Bazerman and Margaret Neale, initial positions "affect each side's perception of what outcomes are possible."[3] Consider this example:

Jake was selling his house on Deer Tail Lake. The house had a unique design, substantial lakefront footage, and many amenities. "If I can get

$350,000, I'll be satisfied. If that's not possible, I'll hold onto it for another year." His agent suggested that he put the house on the market at $395,000, so he did.

In the weeks that followed, Jake's listed price became the anchor point for subsequent negotiations with four potential buyers, all people from outside the area. Three of the four made offers at slightly lower levels—$370,000, $375,000, and $390,000—hoping to make a deal with Jake somewhere in the middle. The fourth, sensing keen competition for the lake house that she wanted badly, offered to pay the full listing price.

This example underscores the effect of anchoring. In the right circumstances, the first party to put a price (or deal package) on the table secures an important psychological advantage. In fact, studies show that negotiation outcomes often correlate to the first offer.

When should you anchor? It may be tactically smart to anchor when you have a reasonably good sense of the other side's reservation price. If you are very uncertain about the other side's reservation price, you might encourage him or her to make the first move.

Where should you place your anchor? In a negotiation in which claiming maximum value is the primary goal, your first offer or proposal should be at or just a bit beyond what you believe is the other side's reservation price, which may be determined through pre-negotiation investigation or through direct probing of the other side. Thus, if you had a sense of Jake's reservation price ($350,000), you might make a first offer at $325,000 and allow him to score some points in negotiating the deal up to $350,000 (assuming you think that amount represents a good and acceptable price).

Wherever you place the anchor, be prepared to articulate *why* your offer or proposal is reasonable or justifiable. "I believe that our listing price of $395,000 is fully justified by the unique qualities of this property, its location, and the high quality of craftsmanship reflected in the building. You'll find that similar properties in this area have been selling at or close to this price."

Anchoring with a price (or a proposal) creates two risks. First, if you are too aggressive, the other side may conclude it will be impossible to make a deal with you. They may also feel personally insulted by your offer. Second, if you've made an erroneous estimate of the other side's reservation price, your offer will be outside the zone of possible agreement. If you fall afoul of either of these risks, have a different line of reasoning ready to support your shift to a less aggressive offer. "Because of the owner's desire to conclude the sale sooner than later, he has authorized me to reduce the price to . . . ."

The best safeguard against making an inept anchoring attempt is preparation prior to negotiations, as described in the previous chapter. If you do your homework, you're much less likely to place an anchor at a point from which you'll be forced to beat an ignominious retreat.

Putting a price or proposal on the table is not the only way to gain advantage through anchoring. If you can define the issues, establish the agenda, or somehow impose your conceptual framework on the debate, you will have accomplished something very similar, and very beneficial to you. Negotiations will then proceed along a path that you have determined.

Counteranchoring

If the other side makes the first offer, you should recognize and resist that offer's potential power as a psychological anchor. Remember that anchors are most powerful when uncertainty is highest—for example, when no one has a clear idea what the price of a company or a piece of equipment should be. When no one has a clue as to the appropriate price, there is no basis for disputing the merits of the first offer.

You can reduce the other side's anchoring power by reducing the uncertainty that surrounds the issue. That means gathering and bringing objective information to the bargaining table.

Don't let the other side set the bargaining range with an anchor unless you think it's a sensible starting point. If you think the anchor suggests an unfavorable or unacceptable starting point, steer the conversation away from numbers and proposals. Focus instead on interests, concerns, and generalities. Then, after some time has passed and more information has surfaced, put *your* number or your proposal on the table, and support it with sound reasoning.

To see how this might be done, let's replay the example of Jake and his lake house. But this time, let's assume that only one potential buyer, Carla, steps forward.

> The real estate agent had just listed Jake's lakefront summer house for $395,000, confident that that number would be a firm anchor point for all incoming bids. But he hadn't counted on dealing with Carla. Carla had had her eye on the lakefront property market in the Deer Tail Lake area for the past two years, so she was familiar with all the current property listings and the dozens that had sold over that time period.
>
> During her first meeting with Jake's agent, Carla explained how she had been tracking property prices on Deer Tail Lake and neighboring lakes for the past two years. Without making any reference to Jake's $395,000 asking price, she cited three sales of comparable properties that had occurred on Deer Tail Lake during the past year, indicating how those properties were more or less similar to Jake's.
>
> "These three are very comparable to your listing in terms of shoreline frontage, lot sizes, and house characteristics," she told the agent as she showed him the listing sheets. "They sold for $325,000, $330,000 and $345,000, respectively, within the past ten months. Factoring in inflation, that makes your client's property worth about $350,000 at the most, which is what I'm prepared to offer you today."

Here, Carla placed her own anchor on the board. Instead of focusing on what Jake wanted from the deal, she ignored his initial price, substituting in its place a new price supported by market data. That relevant data gave her anchor greater authority than Jake's, and made it easier to push his aside. In the absence of other buyers—particularly buyers who hadn't done their homework—Jake and his agent had to deal with Carla in terms of her stated offer. She effectively substituted her anchor for Jake's.

The lesson of this tale is to avoid direct comparison between the other side's initial offer and your own. If the initial offer is not serious or realistic, you can safely ignore it; there's a good chance that the other side will do the same. If the initial offer was serious, and the other side refers to it again, you should respectfully ask them to explain why the offer is reasonable. "Why are you asking for $395,000 in this market? Could you explain how you are justifying that price?"

Be Prepared for Concessionary Moves

Once an anchor point is on the table, the parties generally engage in a set of moves and countermoves that they hope will end in an agreeable price or set of arrangements. For example, if Carla in the previous example offered $350,000 for Jake's lakefront property, Jake more than likely would respond with a counteroffer through his agent, say, $385,000:

> *"We appreciate the research you've done on recent lake property sales, Carla, but we don't feel that the properties you've used as benchmarks are really comparable to Jake's place. After all, he has that big pier and boathouse—and the house itself has been recently renovated. Taking those factors into account, we think that Jake's property is worth substantially more than your offer, and we believe that other buyers will share our view. However, in the interest of getting things wrapped up, Jake is willing to lower his price by $10,000 to $385,000."*

Negotiation experts generally interpret a large concessionary move as an indicator of significant additional flexibility. Give a large concession, and the other side will think that you're capable of making additional large concessions. Thus, Carla may think "If Jake is willing to come down $10,000 in this first counteroffer, he's probably prepared to come down at least another $10,000." A small move, on the other hand, is generally perceived as an indication that the bidding is approaching that party's reservation price, and that further pushing will result in smaller and smaller concessions.

These assumptions are not always true, especially when the other side is in no hurry, and when it has confidence that other parties may come forward with attractive prices or conditions—that is, when it has a strong BATNA. This may be the case in our example. A $10,000 concession on Jake's property isn't a huge concession, even though Carla's bid has satisfied his $350,000 reservation price. We can almost hear Jake's voice as he speaks with his agent over the phone:

"I'm happy that we have an offer of $350,000 already. I could live with that. But we may get a better offer in the next week or so, either from Carla or from another buyer. Actually, I'd expect Carla to up her bid to $360K. If she does that, should we push for a bit more? Should we say, 'Give us $365K and we'll have a deal?' Or should we sit on her offer and hope to get a better one?"

Jake's uncertainty about how far to push Carla in this example is a function of his uncertainty about her BATNA and reservation price. If he could estimate these with confidence, he could drive a harder bargain. In this case, Carla's BATNA may be the price of similar properties on Deer Tail Lake or other nearby lakes. He could ask his agent to come up with a list of other similar properties on those lakes. Those might represent the set of Carla's alternatives.

The best advice about concessions is to avoid the impulse to make them. Few of us like negotiating, so we want to get it over as quickly as possible. And as social creatures we want other people to like us, and to view us as reasonable. These factors often make inexperienced negotiators too ready to make concessions. If you find yourself in this category, here are a few tips:

- Look to your BATNA before you consider making a concession. If your BATNA is very strong (especially relative to the other side's), a concession may be unnecessary in making a deal.

- If you're impatient to get it over with because negotiating is stressful, take a break before you consider a concession. If the other side is expecting a $10,000 concession on the price of the home you're selling, think about how difficult it was for you to earn that $10,000. Think about the good things you could do with the $10,000 the other side would like you to give away. Ask yourself, "Is getting rid of a little stress worth $10,000?"

- If your need to be liked or seen as a reasonable person is urging you to make a concession, forget about it. The other side is more likely to view you as a chump or an easy mark if you concede too readily. Remember, too, that deal making isn't about making friends.

The Ticking Clock

In a buyer-seller negotiation, such as the Jake and Carla example, time can be an important tool. From the buyer's perspective, the seller should never be allowed to feel that he can indefinitely sit on the buyer's most recent bid while he awaits a better offer. The seller will simply use the offer to improve his BATNA. The remedy is to attach an expiration date to the offer to buy. Negotiators sometimes refer to this tactic as an *exploding offer.* If Carla decided to counter Jake's latest offer ($385,000) with a bid of $360,000, she might stipulate that "this offer is good until 9 P.M. on this coming Saturday, September 23." That expiration date would put a fire under Jake and force him to make a decision. In the absence of an expiration date, Jake would simply tell himself, "Now that I have an option to sell at $360,000, I can wait for a better offer."

Package Options for a Favorable Deal

Offering alternative proposals (two or more) is often an effective deal-making tactic. Consider this example:

> Joe is negotiating with Robert and Sharon for the purchase of their small sailboat and trailer. The trailer is of minimal importance to Joe because he expects to secure a permanent mooring. But it wouldn't be a bad thing to own, as he may have to tow the boat some day. So he makes alternative proposals: "I'm willing to pay $18,000 for the boat and trailer as a package, or $16,000 for the boat alone. You could sell the trailer separately. What's your preference?"

Package options have dual benefits. First, people don't like to feel pushed into a corner. A single proposal may feel like an ultimatum—take it or leave it. But when presented with alternative proposals, people may compare the proposals to each other instead of to their original goals. In addition, when the other negotiators won't discuss their interests, you can often infer them by noticing which proposal they prefer.

Before presenting alternative proposals, however, do the following:

- Assess the value of each option to each side.

- Consider whether the diminution of one option would be off-set by an enhancement of another.

- If you prefer one of the alternatives, adjust at least one of the proposals so that you feel equally positive about at least two of them.

Closing the Deal

Assuming that things go well, you'll eventually reach a point where you're fairly satisfied with the negotiation and you want to wrap things up. The other side may or may not be at the same point. Here are four recommended steps for closing the deal:

1. **Signal the end of the road before you get there.** If you have been negotiating back and forth, showing flexibility on various issues, and then suddenly announce you're at your bottom line, you are likely to be challenged or not taken seriously. So as you approach the parameters of what you would like in a final deal, say so. Repeat the warning, not as a threat but as a courtesy, particularly if the other negotiator seems to expect a lot more movement in his or her direction.

2. **Allow flexibility if you anticipate going beyond the final round.** If you are aware that the other negotiator lacks final authority, leave yourself some flexibility, or wiggle room, in the final terms. More specifically, don't give the other side your best and last offer—save that in case you have to bend during the final round. However:

   - Don't create so much flexibility that the deal will be rejected by the other side's decision maker.
   - Consider whatever final trade you would be willing to make if you end up requesting significant adjustment in the final terms.

3. **Discourage the other side from seeking further concessions.** If you appear to have reached a final deal that is acceptable to the

other side (and perhaps also favorable to you), discourage further tweaking in their favor.

- Express your willingness to accept the total package, without changes.
- Explain that adjustment in their favor on one term would have to be balanced by adjustment in your favor on another. For example, "If we open that issue, then I'm afraid we'll have to reopen the whole deal for it to work for me."

4. **Write down the terms.** If your negotiation time has been well spent, don't risk ruining it by failing to record and sign your agreement. People's memories of their agreement will inevitably diverge; recording the terms of the agreement avoids future disputes and confusion. It also provides closure.

Even if counsel will draft the official documents, write an informal agreement in principle. Decide whether it is binding or not, and say so in the document. Even if your informal agreement is nonbinding, it will serve as a common reference by both parties as future, good-faith questions arise.

Tactics for Integrative Negotiations

Integrative negotiations, as described in chapter 1, are those in which the parties enlarge the pie through trades. These negotiations require a different set of tactics, beginning with a slower, more exploratory opening. They rely on greater collaboration and information exchange. Unlike the win-lose tactics described earlier, where the focus is on claiming value, integrative deals aim to create *and* claim value.

Getting Started

As you begin your negotiations, don't start with the numbers. Instead, talk and listen. Observe the suggestions offered earlier in the section "Making a Good Start" and the "Tips" box regarding setting the right tone. They apply equally here. Frame the task positively, as a joint endeavor from which both sides should expect to benefit. Emphasize your openness to the other side's interests and concerns.

As you learn about the other side's concerns and interests, don't make a proposal too quickly; a premature offer won't benefit from information gleaned during the negotiation process itself. If you are the buyer, such information could alert you to the seller's desperate financial situation, thereby leading you to make a lower initial offer than you otherwise might have. On the other hand, the information could reveal that the seller is not desperate at all, thereby preventing you from making a low initial offer that might insult the seller.

Instead of hastily throwing out an offer, try these techniques:

- Ask open-ended questions about the other side's needs, interests, concerns, and goals.

- Probe the other side's willingness to *trade off* one thing for another. For example, "Do you care more about X or Y?"

- Inquire about the other side's underlying interests by asking why certain conditions—for example, a particular delivery date—are important.

- Listen closely to the other side's responses without jumping in to cross-examine, correct, or object.

- Be an active listener. The more they talk, the more information you're likely to get.

- Express empathy for the other side's perspective, needs, and interests. Empathy is especially important in highly charged situations. It takes active listening one step further, confirming that you can connect with the speaker and the underlying tensions or emotional issues.

- Adjust your assumptions based on what you've learned. The assumptions that you've made about the other side's interests and circumstances when preparing for the negotiation may be wrong, in which case you'll need to revisit your strategy.

- Be forthcoming about your own business needs, interests, and concerns. It is just as important to assert what you need and want (and why) as it is to listen carefully to the other side. Indeed, striking a balance between empathy and assertiveness is essential to effective negotiating. If you are too empathetic and insufficiently assertive, you may shortchange your own interests. If you are too assertive and insufficiently empathetic, you risk missing a deal and escalating emotions. But don't barrage the other side with all of your interests and concerns at once.

- Work to create a two-way exchange of information. Stay flexible about who asks questions and who states concerns first. If

Tips for Active Listening

There's a big difference between keeping your mouth shut while the other party is talking and what communication experts refer to as "active" listening. Active listening helps you capture what the other side has to say while signaling that you are alert and eager to hear what the other side has on its mind. Here are some tips for being an active listener. They will help you in any type of negotiation.

- Keep your eyes on the speaker.

- Take notes as appropriate.

- Don't allow yourself to think about anything but what the speaker is saying.

- Resist the urge to formulate your response until *after* the speaker has finished.

- Pay attention to the speaker's body language.

- Ask questions to get more information and to encourage the speaker to continue.

- Repeat in your own words what you've heard to ensure that you understand and to let the speaker know that you've processed his or her words.

the other side seems uncomfortable with your initial questions, offer to talk about one or two of your most important points— and explain why they are important.

- Continue your relationship-building efforts even after the negotiating has begun. Show empathy, respect, and courtesy throughout the proceedings. Always remember that the other side consists of human beings with feelings, limits, and vulnerabilities.

- Refrain from personal attacks. Don't accuse or blame. Maintain a sense of humor.

- When an issue seems to make another negotiator tense, acknowledge the thorniness of the issue.

- Don't feel pressured to close a deal too quickly. Instead, generate options that offer mutual gain.

Look for Options That Exploit Differences

During the negotiation, you are confronted with the other side's positions and come to understand the interests underlying those positions. It is hoped that the other side will understand your positions and interests just as well. The challenge now is to arrive at an outcome that satisfies both parties' interests. One place to look for a mutually satisfying outcome is in the differences between the parties.

People know intuitively to build upon their shared interests. Less obvious sources of value are in the differences between them. By trading on differences, you create value that neither party could have created on its own. In particular, look for differences in these places:

- **Access to resources.** For example, Martha, who owns both a retail store and a restaurant, is negotiating with an interior designer for his services in renovating the restaurant. She agrees to pay a somewhat higher price than planned for the restaurant design in exchange for the designer ordering fixtures and furnishings for the retail store at his trade discount. The owner would not otherwise have ready access to these discounts—yet providing them costs the designer nothing. Value has been created for both sides.

- **Future expectations.** For example, the current owner of a business is selling. He demands a high price because he predicts that the market for his product will increase over time. The potential buyer is unwilling to pay that high price; she does not share the owner's rosy outlook. Within this difference of opinion, they see an opportunity. They agree to a base sale price, plus 20 percent of the company's increased revenues over the next five years—if any—with the current owner providing advice and assisting with marketing and distribution plans over that period. Under this arrangement, the buyer will get a lower price and the seller will be able to capture the upside growth in the business he anticipates.

- **Time preference.** The timing of a deal can be a barrier to a mutually satisfactory conclusion. For example, Jonathan is happy with the CEO's plan to promote him to vice president of marketing, but unhappy that he must play a waiting role until the incumbent retires six months hence. The CEO, however, has arranged for the current marketing VP to use that time to finalize the company's strategic distribution agreement with its dealers. "He engineered this strategy and has close personal ties to key players on the other side. I want him to conclude the deal." Within these differences, however, the CEO finds a solution: He will put Jonathan in charge of a team that is working on the plan to implement the new distribution contract. That satisfies Jonathan and benefits the company.

- **Risk aversion.** What is highly risky for one party is often less risky for another. Parties often have different risk tolerances. In these cases, value can be created by shifting risk to the party better able to bear it—in exchange, of course, for higher potential returns for the party assuming the risk. For example, Jeff and Jessica are negotiating with Jones Properties, a developer, for the purchase of a newly built condominium. For Jeff and Jessica, newcomers to the housing market, the condo would be by far their largest investment. "What if I got transferred and had to sell sometime soon?" Jeff ponders. "If the condo market were depressed at the time of sale, we'd take a heavy loss." Jones Properties, on the other hand, owns hundreds of properties in dozens of buildings scattered around the country. Its risk of ownership is highly diversified. And so it poses a solution: As part of the sales agreement, it will agree to buy back Jeff and Jessica's condo at any time within two years of purchase at 95 percent of the purchase price less transaction costs.

Take Your Time

Don't be tempted to close the deal too quickly—when the first acceptable proposal is on the table but little information has been exchanged. Spend a bit more time finding a deal that is better for both sides. Signal that the proposal on the table is worth considering, but also state that it may be improved by learning more about your respective interests and concerns. Then, begin the search for mutually beneficial options.

Here are a few more suggestions for generating integrative solutions:

- Move from a particular issue to a more general description of the problem, then to theoretical solutions, and finally back to the specific issue.

- Pay special attention to shared interests and opportunities for cooperation.

- Consider joint brainstorming with the other side—it can be a very fruitful way of generating creative alternatives. Set ground rules that encourage the participants to express any and all ideas, no matter how wild or impractical. Be careful not to criticize or express disapproval of any suggestion. At this stage, such judgments inhibit creativity, making people reluctant to make further suggestions—and more likely to criticize any ideas you volunteer as well.

General Tactics: Framing and Continual Evaluation

Whether you're engaged in a distributive or integrative negotiation, your results will be better if you adopt any one of the three following tactics: framing, process moves, and continual evaluation. These tactics may be used at or away from the table. Process moves were discussed in chapter 3, so this section focuses on the other two tactics.

Framing

Fill a glass of water halfway to the top. Now, if you described this glass to someone else, would you say it was half empty or half full? Whichever way you describe the glass, you are framing the situation. If the other person accepts that frame without question, subsequent discussion will proceed within that frame. This could be advantageous to you. Consider these examples.

- *The glass is half empty.* A labor negotiator tries to frame upcoming wage and benefit talks with a company.

  "During the past three years, hard work by our members has helped this company to triple its revenues and almost double its profits. Management salaries have grown substantially as a result, and key executives have rewarded themselves with record-breaking bonuses. And what is management willing to share with rank-and-file employees? A mere 25 percent increase in wages over the next three years! That, we contend, is a slap in the face to the people who have created this company's good fortunes."

  In other words, a fair sharing of the wealth created by the employees should frame negotiations.

- *The glass is half full.* Management makes its pitch to labor.

  "We are pleased to offer our rank-and-file employees a salary increase of 25 percent over the next three years. That increase is one-third higher than what our main market competitors have offered their employees. It will put the average annual wage of our people some $3,000 above the industry average, and will allow the company to retain sufficient funds to reinvest in the technology it needs to ensure job security and future wage increases."

  In other words, wage negotiations should be made with a frame that emphasizes financial constraints and the company's desire to ensure job security and higher future incomes.

Sequine   Like an anchor, a frame can determine how negotiations will
ensue. It orients the parties and encourages them to examine the issues within a defined perspective. The labor union frame just offered
would put management on the defensive and encourage negotiations around a framework that stressed "fair distribution" of the
profit pie. The management frame is based on its generosity relative
to peer group companies and the benefits workers may receive in the
future thanks to profit reinvestment. (Note how the company has
used external criteria—as described in the previous chapter—to establish the fairness and reasonableness of its offer.) Whichever side
can get the other to buy into its frame will have a negotiating advantage. As Bazerman and Neale put it, the way in which options
available in a negotiation are framed, or presented, can strongly affect
a party's willingness to reach an agreement.[4]

Effective framing taps into preexisting mental models of how we
should behave under various conditions. Thus, how one side frames
a solution can determine how others decide to behave. Marjorie
Corman Aaron, a consultant and trainer with many years of experience in mediation, negotiation, and dispute resolution, gives the example of a bank officer faced with demands by local community
activists to provide more generous lending arrangements. In advising
the bank's board on a course of action, the officer could adopt any
one of several frames:

> He could frame the demands to the board of directors as a "shake-
> down," thereby invoking a mental model that resists "knuckling under
> to pressure." But if he framed it as a business problem—the need to
> earn the goodwill of the community—the board might be persuaded to
> fund some programs. If he framed the bank's circumstances as "wrestling
> with a 500-pound gorilla," the board would probably do whatever it
> would take to get the gorilla off its back, and quickly.[5]

So, if you frame your position in terms of a mental model the other
side can embrace, you'll have less trouble moving toward agreement.

More generally, you can use these frames:

- Frame your proposal in terms that represent a gain instead of a
  loss. Instead of saying "My current offer is only 10 percent less

than what you are asking," say "I've already increased my offer by 10 percent."

- Tap into people's natural aversion to risk. Risk aversion has two consequences:

  1. People who are very risk averse will often accept larger potential losses in the future rather than incur smaller losses today. This explains why many people will seek remedies in court and possibly suffer paying a larger settlement in the future rather than pay a smaller settlement today.

  2. Most people prefer a bird in the hand rather than two in the bush. In other words, they prefer the certainty of a smaller offer to the uncertainty of a larger future gain. "I know that you want $400,000 for that property, and you may get it someday. However, I'm willing to pay $340,000 for it today. Can we make a deal?"

Continual Evaluation and Preparation

Normally we think of negotiating as a linear process of preparation, negotiation, and eventual agreement or failure. The first step takes place away from the table; the rest take place at the table. In simple interactions, this model often holds true. But many other negotiations are complex and can take place in succeeding rounds and involve several different parties. New information can appear at various points, casting new light on the issues at stake. Different parties can offer concessions or heighten their demands. This more complex dynamic suggests a nonlinear approach to the preparation process, as shown in figure 4-1. Here preparation is followed by negotiation, which produces outcomes and information that require evaluation. The outputs of evaluation then feed into a new round of preparation and subsequent negotiation. Round and round it goes until agreement is reached or the parties call it quits.

Michael Watkins, author and expert on the subject of negotiations, suggests that the ambiguities and uncertainties associated with complex deals should caution negotiators to give less attention to

FIGURE 4-1

Nonlinear Negotiating Process

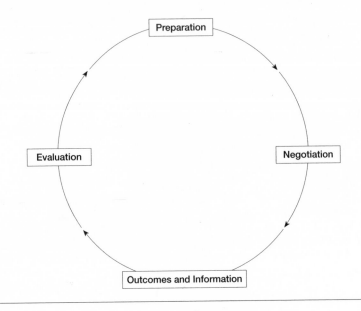

pre-negotiation preparation and more attention to what he calls "planning to learn." Learning must be ongoing. After all, the information available to negotiators before going to the table is bound to be limited and may even be inaccurate.

So instead of setting your course based on pre-negotiation information, consider doing the following:

- Take small steps, gathering better information as you proceed.

- Continually learn from new information and the behavior of the other side.

- Use that learning to adjust and readjust your course as you move forward.

Evaluation is another important element of the process, and should be part of your tactics. Periodically, you should put a little distance between yourself and the negotiations and ask: How are things going? Are negotiations proceeding along a track that will eventually serve my goals? Are they playing my game, or am I playing theirs? Whose frame dominates the talks? If I were representing the other side, how would I answer these same questions?

Answering these questions objectively isn't natural or easy. A person must take the perspective of a neutral stranger and adopt an outside-looking-in stance. This is essential to mastering the game.

Summing Up

The first challenge in negotiation is to get the other side to the table. This won't happen unless the other side sees that it is better off negotiating than going with the status quo. Encourage negotiation by offering incentives, making the status quo expensive, and by enlisting the help of allies.

Once you've gotten the other side to the table, get things off to a good start by relieving tension, making sure that all parties agree with the agenda and the process, and setting the right tone.

Several tactics are particularly useful in distributed (or win-lose) deals:

- Establish an anchor, an initial position around which negotiations make adjustments.

- If an initial anchor is unacceptable to you, steer the conversation away from numbers and proposals. Focus instead on interests, concerns, and generalities. Then, after some time has passed and more information has surfaced, put *your* number or proposal on the table, and support it with sound reasoning.

- Make concessionary moves if you must. But remember, many interpret a large concessionary move as an indicator that you're capable of conceding still more. A small concession, on the other hand, is generally seen as an indication that the bidding is approaching the reservation price and that any succeeding concessions will be smaller and smaller.

Tactics for integrative (win–win) negotiations are fundamentally different from those just described since value creation is one of the goals. So concentrate on these tactics:

- Active listening

- Exploiting complementary interests

- Packaging options for more favorable deals

Finally, the chapter offered tactics useable in any context:

- Framing

- Continual evaluation

5

Frequently Asked Tactical Questions

Answers You Need

Key Topics Covered in This Chapter

- *Tactics regarding price*

- *Tactics regarding process*

- *Tactics regarding people*

T HE PREVIOUS CHAPTER described tactics you can use in various types of negotiations. This chapter follows up with answers to frequently asked questions (FAQs) about negotiating tactics.[1] For convenience, questions and answers are organized under three broad categories: price, procedures, and people.

FAQs About Price

Should I ever state my acceptable range?

Some negotiators will ask you to state a monetary range of what you're willing to pay. Do not comply. This would give away your reservation price. For example, if you tell someone that you would pay $20,000 to $25,000 for a piece of property, rest assured that you will pay *at least* $25,000. The other side will think, "That's the reservation price," and it is the only number he or she will pay attention to. It is much better to work in terms of your bottom line, or "the best I can do."

The only reason to mention a range occurs toward the end of the negotiating process, to discourage the other side from pushing you beyond it. For example, after several rounds of back and forth on a dollar figure, you are at $23,000, and the other side is at $30,000 and seems to be pushing for a deal at $28,000. You could say, "My range walking in here today was $20,000 to $23,000, but not above

$25,000." Revealing your range may make it easier for the seller to accept $25,000 because he will feel that he has pushed you to the top.

Should I ever tell the other side my real bottom line?

You can reveal your bottom line, but only if you've reached it (or are about to). If you do reveal your bottom line, make sure you call it just that, with appropriate emphasis or firmness. Otherwise, the other side may not take you seriously, and may view that number or proposal as just another step on the way to a final deal.

Suppose that the other side opens with an incredibly unreasonable number. Should I counter with an equally unreasonable number, or decline to counter at all?

Consider one of the following strategies:

- Make a joke to indicate that you don't consider the other side's number a serious offer: "Right, and the moon is made of green cheese. Now, let's get serious."
- Clearly state that the other side's number is entirely out of the range you had imagined for the deal. Go back to talking about interests. Ask about a specific issue of some importance. Explain your perspective on the deal—how it might have value to you or others similarly situated. (You will, of course, be describing value that falls in an entirely different ballpark.) Let some time and discussion go by. Then you might suggest a number or proposal that you can justify as reasonable and that is in the favorable end of your range (or close to what you estimate their reservation price is, whichever is better). Do *not* refer to their initial number or proposal. Ignore it. If you counter with an equally unreasonable number, you will either contribute to the impasse or make the road to agreement longer and more difficult.
- Indicate that the offer is entirely out of range. Then express your concern that a deal may not be possible. Try to get the other side to bid against itself as follows: "That offer is so low

that we will not even consider it. Why don't you confer with your people and get back to me with something more realistic? I'll be in my office all afternoon."

faire un'offerte + dette

FAQs About Process

Is it ever acceptable to bid against myself—to make two moves in a row?

It's not a good idea. Just say, "Wait, you seem to be asking me to make another move here. I made the last offer; I don't want to bid against myself. Give me your offer." This usually elicits at least a token move on the other side.

If it doesn't, if they are stuck and the only way to make progress is for you to move again, you should announce your awareness of what you are doing, and state that it should not be considered a precedent. Make your next move in good faith, to a proposal or number you can justify as reasonable, explain your reasoning, and ask the other side to do the same. If they don't, you may have reached an impasse.

To bridge the gap, consider broadening the discussion of the parties' interests, and formulating other creative options, perhaps through joint brainstorming. You might bring in a third-party facilitator.

Is it smart or fair to bluff?

Is it okay to bluff or puff during a negotiation? Sure. One man's puff is another's positive spin. One woman's bluff is another's best foot forward. Lying about a material fact, however, is almost certainly grounds for legal action. In certain circumstances, creating a false impression or failing to disclose material information may be a formal legal breach. Nevertheless, as long as what you bring to the table has real value, you need not reveal all the circumstances that make you willing to conclude a deal. Thus, if you are negotiating the terms of a job offer, there is nothing wrong with describing the major projects for which you have been responsible and your likely next step on the corporate ladder in your current company. There is no shame in describing your achievements in a positive light. You need not mention that the new division president is impossible to deal with.

In a complex deal, is it better to reach agreement issue by issue or wait until the end?

Every deal is different, but it's generally better to aim for tentative agreements, or agreed-upon ranges, for each issue, one at a time. This will give you the necessary flexibility to make value-creating trade-offs between issues later on and to create alternative packages of different options. The risk of negotiating each issue in serial fashion is that you lose opportunities to create value through trades.

Is it better to deal with difficult or easy issues first?

In general, dealing with easier issues will build momentum, deepen the parties' commitment to the process, and enable the parties to become familiar with each other's negotiation and communication styles before hitting the tough stuff.

In some instances, however, you may want to deal with a more difficult issue as a threshold matter. If you cannot reach tentative agreement on the difficult issues, then you will not have wasted time on the smaller issues. It is also true that once the most difficult issue is resolved, smaller issues often fall more easily into place.

What if there is an unexpected turn in the road—before or after an agreement?

Unexpected developments can endanger potential agreements. They can also undermine agreements already made. Consider this example:

You have entered a fixed price contract with a general contractor to build new office suites and conference rooms in an older brick building purchased by your company. The suites and conference rooms are to be paneled in a lovely pear wood. But after the contract is signed, a pear wood blight is discovered, which triples the cost of pear wood.

Under your negotiated agreement, the contractor is to bear the risk of fluctuation in material costs. If you insist on that term, the contractor may try to make up some of the cost in other ways, perhaps by shorting the detail work. If you agree to renegotiate, absorbing some or all of the additional cost (or choosing a different wood), the contractor is more likely to do a high-quality job.

The next month, you discover that the bottom floor of the building is sinking and walls are cracking because of settling in the foundation. This was not part of the original contract, but you want the contractor to take it on as soon as possible and at a reasonable price. What goes around comes around.

Similar events can happen while you're in the process of negotiating a deal. In both cases, analyze how the unexpected development affects the decision to go forward. Determine if a deal still makes sense, or if you need to undo the deal that has been negotiated. Also:

- Contact the negotiator(s) on the other side immediately.
- Acknowledge the unexpected nature of what has happened.
- Affirm your commitment to working on the problem (if that is so).
- Jointly discuss the underlying principles and intent of the deal as originally negotiated, and agree upon what issues or provisions are affected.
- Pick up the negotiations again.

FAQs About People Problems

What happens when you pit a collaborative negotiator against a positional hard bargainer?

A positional bargainer aims to win at the other side's expense. He will agree that "compromise is what will get us to a deal," then expect all the compromises to come from the other side.

An effective collaborative negotiator should be able to deal with this type of negotiator if she recognizes the situation for what it is. After all, she will have analyzed her BATNA, set a reservation price, and considered both opening and first-offer strategies. If the positional hard bargainer refuses to disclose information and begins to use any disclosures against the cooperative bargainer, that's a clear signal that this is not likely to be a win–win proposition. The negotiator should seek reciprocity or refrain from providing additional information.

The real question is whether the collaborative negotiator will be able to "convert" the hard bargainer, at least sufficiently to create some value in the deal. The answer is "maybe." If the collaborative negotiator is effective and resourceful, she should be able to tease out some of the interests underlying the hard bargainer's positions. She may then suggest different options and packages for meeting both parties' interests. Even the most recalcitrant hard bargainer can recognize when it benefits his interests to join in creating value.

How should I respond if the other side seeks to change something in its offer after a deal has been reached?

Chances are the other side is afflicted with the *winner's curse:* Whenever they reach a deal, they are cursed with the thought that they could have gotten more.

If the other side tries to change one item, express surprise or disappointment. Explain that if they must make a change, then they must understand that you will want to open up other issues as well. "I agreed to a total package. A change on one issue affects the entire package. Are you willing to renegotiate other issues?" If the answer is yes, then the other side was sincere, and you should proceed with the renegotiation. If they reconsider and withdraw the request for a change, then assume that they were just testing you. If they insist that they must have this change and no others, express dismay, then decide whether the adjusted deal has sufficient value for you to agree.

What should I do when the negotiator on the other side has a temper tantrum?

Don't respond in kind. Instead, help him regain control. The right response will depend upon how angry or upset you feel, the value of the deal, and whether it is your choice to proceed. Here are some alternatives:

- Sit quietly. Say nothing. After a few moments, resume the negotiation with a calm voice.
- Stop. Say, "This is getting us nowhere. I'm inclined to leave
  and let you cool off. Is that what you want?"

If his shouting was intended to get you upset and off-balance,
you certainly shouldn't reward that strategy by negotiating in that
less-than-top-form condition. Also, keep in mind that you have some
control over who you will deal with. Consider contacting someone
else on the other side to suggest that another negotiator be assigned
to the deal.

I don't believe what the other side is saying. What should I do?

You suspect the other side is lying or *bluffing*. At best, they're just
telling you what they think is needed for an agreement, and have no
intention of following through on their promises. Here's how you
could respond:

- Make sure they understand that the deal is predicated on
  their accurate and truthful representation of the situation. For
  example: "If you can't provide shipping on the schedule
  we've described, it's best to tell me right now."
- Require that they provide back-up documentation, and that
  the deal be explicitly contingent on its accuracy.
- Insist on enforcement mechanisms, such as a penalty for noncompliance (or perhaps positive incentives for early performance). Example: "We expect the final agreement to contain
  a late fee of $1,000 per day for every day that construction
  milestones are not met. On the other hand, we are willing to
  pay you a bonus of $20,000 if you can have the building ready
  for occupancy on or before July 20 of the coming year."

**When, if ever, is it appropriate to negotiate over the telephone or by
e-mail? Or is it essential to insist on a face-to-face meeting?**

It is far better to negotiate face to face when personal, nonverbal
cues matter. For example, is this a deal in which the other side might

be tempted to lie or shade the truth? Are the parties professionally or emotionally invested in what's at stake? These situations often reveal themselves through nonverbal cues.

Some research indicates that people are less likely to lie in person, perhaps because they fear that the other side will detect their deception. Indeed, in a face-to-face negotiation we see the sideways glances of the other negotiating team, we sense when they are becoming uncomfortable, and we pick up the nonverbal cues that indicate something is more important than their words indicate.

Anecdotal evidence indicates that e-mail or other written messages may have a greater tendency to result in disputes and impasses. The person who receives an e-mail (or fax) may interpret a comment negatively when the sender did not intend it that way. Because the sender is not there to read the facial expression or hear the exclamation of the recipient, he or she can't correct the impression. The original sender is surprised and feels unjustifiably attacked when the return message carries a nasty tone, and responds in kind.

On the other hand, e-mail communication is devoid of emotions. For an inexperienced negotiator, this can be a big plus. He or she is less likely to be emotionally whipsawed by an aggressive negotiator on the other side. And since e-mail makes it possible to reflect on a message before hitting the Send button, one is less likely to give away vital information to the other side. Unwarranted disclosure can be a problem in face-to-face discussions. Some people talk too much. Either through thoughtlessness or an effort to make themselves seem important, they give away vital information. The chance of doing this is lessened when e-mail is the medium of communication.

Some, but not all, of these problems of e-mail are partially solved by using the telephone. You can use and interpret tone of voice to keep communications on track. However, it is more cumbersome to propose creative ideas. You can't put them on a chalkboard or easel. And some recent research indicates that people are more likely to bluff over the telephone. On the other hand, if the negotiation is over a simple issue, where personal communication is not likely to matter, the most efficient method works best.

Determining Authority

The appendix contains a handy worksheet that will help determine and confirm the authority level you have and the authority level of the person or persons with whom you will be negotiating. An interactive version of this worksheet is available on the Harvard Business Essentials Web site: www.elearning.hbsp.org/businesstools.

How should I react when the other side challenges my credentials, status, or authority to make a deal?

Why are they challenging you? Are they just trying to make you defensive, put you off-balance? Or do they have genuine concerns?

The best approach is to shift the discussion to general ground rules. Say something like this: "Right. We should be clear about whose approval is needed for a deal—both on my side *and* yours. I am authorized to complete the deal within these parameters: *x, y,* and *z.* I need formal approval for any agreements outside those parameters. Now, what about you? What are you authorized to do?"

If the challenge to your authority was posed to make you feel defensive, you will have demonstrated that such strategies will not be successful.

6

Barriers to Agreement

How to Recognize and Overcome Them

Key Topics Covered in This Chapter

- *Die-hard bargainers*

- *Lack of trust*

- *Informational vacuums and the negotiator's dilemma*

- *Structural impediments*

- *Spoilers*

- *Cultural and gender differences*

- *Communication problems*

- *The power of dialogue*

SOME NEGOTIATIONS cannot be completed for the simple reason that one or another party has better alternatives elsewhere. For them, negotiations are not in their best interest; it's better to walk away. But other negotiations for which ZOPAs exist nonetheless fail. One need only examine geopolitical history to note the many conflicts that could have been negotiated successfully had the parties been more objective and less driven by pride, impatience, stubbornness, or ignorance of the facts. The same happens in business and interpersonal negotiations. This chapter examines barriers to successful negotiations and how they can be overcome or eliminated.

Die–Hard Bargainers

They are out there: the die-hard bargainers, for whom every negotiation is a test of wills and a battle for every scrap of value. Unless you're willing to play the same game—or lack other options—negotiations with these people may be fruitless. Here are some ways of making the most of this type of situation:

- Recognize the game they're playing, and don't be thrown off-balance by it. Anticipate low-ball offers, grudging concessions, and lots of bluffing and puffing along the way. Don't let these antics prevent you from analyzing your BATNA and setting your reservation price and aspirations. Try to assess theirs, and proceed accordingly.

- Because you're dealing with highly acquisitive people, be guarded in the information you disclose. These people will take whatever information you reveal and use it against you—and give nothing in return. So, disclose only the information that cannot be used to exploit you.

- If you're unsure about the attitude of the other side, test their willingness to share information. Let slip a minor piece of information and see what they do with it. Do they use it against you? Do they respond by offering information to you? If the answer is "yes" to the first question and "no" to the second, be guarded with any further information.

- Try a different tack. Suggest alternative options: "Here are two alternatives for solving this problem." Ask which they prefer, and why. That will throw the ball into their court, tempting them to respond. If they won't respond, ask if it would be better or worse for them if you added or eliminated one of the options. Continue in this manner. The idea is to get the other side to show more of its hand.

- Be willing to walk away. If the other side sees a clear benefit in reaching an agreement, it will be less overbearing if it knows that its behavior creates the risk of no deal at all.

- Strengthen your BATNA. If your position is weak, the other side can bully or ignore you with little risk. But if your BATNA is strong—or growing stronger over time—the other side will be more respectful of your interests. (See "Speak Softly but Build Your BATNA.")

Speak Softly but Build Your BATNA

In the years following the French Revolution, tensions mounted between France's new government (the Directory) and the fledgling United States. The Directory closed French ports to U.S. shipping, and its navy captured many American trade vessels in what became known as the Quasi-War. Envoys sent to Paris to negotiate a peaceful relationship and open trade were turned away.

The Quasi-War at sea, and popular revulsion at the murderous excesses of the revolution, turned American opinion against its former ally, and many clamored for war. President John Adams stood squarely against the urge to declare war, seeing only danger and damage in such a move. He sought, instead, a peaceful settlement of disputes and a resumption of trade, and he kept up a diplomatic campaign over several years to secure both.

France had clear advantages in its dispute with the United States. It needed U.S. friendship and trade much less than the United States needed the same from France. And once Napoleon Bonaparte came to power, France became the most formidable military power in the Western world. It could afford to treat the small North American country in high-handed fashion—and it did.

Undeterred, Adams kept pushing for negotiations. But at the same time he strengthened his position (i.e., his BATNA) by building up the American navy from a handful of vessels to fifty ships, including state-of-the-art frigates. That maritime clout helped break the impasse. "Adam's insistence on American naval strength," wrote biographer David McCollough, "proved decisive in achieving peace with France" in 1800.[1] A century later, another American president, Theodore Roosevelt, followed Adams's example, summing up his diplomatic approach with the slogan "Speak softly but carry a big stick."

Lack of Trust

Agreements are difficult in the absence of mutual trust. "How can we negotiate with these people?" is a common refrain. "We cannot believe a thing they tell us. And if we were to make a deal, how could we be sure that they'd hold up their end of the bargain?"

The importance of trust was cited by Dominick Misino, a retired New York Police Department hostage negotiator, in the *Harvard Business Review*. Trust, he said, begins with civility and respect:

> *When I'm dealing with an armed criminal, for example, my first rule of thumb is simply to be polite. . . . A lot of times, the people I'm dealing with are extremely nasty. And the reason for this is that their anxiety level is so high: A guy armed and barricaded in a bank is in a fight-or-flight mode. To defuse the situation, I've got to try to understand what's going on in his head. The first step to getting there is to show him respect, which shows my sincerity and reliability. So before the bad guy demands anything, I always ask him if he needs something.*[2]

The sincerity and reliability cited by Misino are the building blocks of trust.

Given the choice of negotiating with an untrustworthy party, people with realistic options will turn to their alternatives, or they will hedge the agreements they make with these parties by making them more narrow or limited than they would otherwise be. Negotiation scholars refer to these as *insecure agreements*. But don't give up too quickly if you suspect the other side is not entirely trustworthy.

- Emphasize that the deal is predicated on their accurate and truthful representation of the situation.

- Require that they provide back-up documentation, and that the terms of the deal be explicitly contingent on the documentation's accuracy.

- Structure the agreement in a way that makes future benefits contingent on current compliance and performance.

- Insist on compliance transparency. *Compliance transparency* refers
  to one's ability to monitor compliance from the outside. You
  want to craft a compliance mechanism that is readily monitored
  and that assures you that terms of the agreement are being hon-
  ored by the other side. For example, if you've agreed to license
  a proprietary technology in return for royalty payments, you'd
  be wise to build into the agreement your stated right to examine the other side's books on a regular basis to ensure the
  proper calculation of royalties.

- Require enforcement mechanisms, such as a security deposit,
  escrow arrangement, or penalties for noncompliance (or perhaps positive incentives for early performance).

You can also help to foster a climate of greater trust by building
relationships between people and by improving the channels of communication between the organizations involved in the negotiations.
Joint ventures, for instance, require substantial trust between independent organizations. Experienced managers of joint ventures give
key personnel of the different parties opportunities to know each other
and to collaborate in making decisions. They arrange meetings within
which problems, opportunities, and working frictions can be communicated and addressed. These mechanisms create opportunities for
creating the trust needed for the success of the venture.

Informational Vacuums
and the Negotiator's Dilemma

Negotiators have difficulty in connecting with each other when they
have little or no pertinent information about the interests of their
counterparts. In the absence of illuminating information, they pass by
each other like ships sailing in darkness. Consider this example:

> *Peabody Products had just won a big contract from the Royal Navy to
> produce electric motors over the next twelve months and was scrambling
> to set up the necessary supplier relationships. Among the things it*

needed were 20,000 wiring harnesses, and it needed them in a hurry. Unfortunately, all of its regular suppliers were backlogged with other work. Then the procurement department found Western Manufacturing, a small component producer located outside Glasgow.

Neither of the two companies knew much about the other, and their negotiators had reasons for not sharing certain information. For example, Peabody's representatives didn't want Western's people to know how desperate they were to get 20,000 wiring harnesses in short order. Without them, their deal with the Royal Navy might founder. "If the people at Western knew this," said one company official, "we'd be in a poor bargaining position and bound to get gouged on the price. They'd know that they had us over a barrel." The people at Western likewise felt that they were in a poor bargaining position. "If Peabody Products were to learn that we are operating at forty percent capacity," said Western's sales manager to his boss, "they'd demand a rock-bottom price— and we'd probably give it."

Though Peabody and Western need each other for important business reasons, neither realizes it. Each fears to reveal information about its situation. And if neither party speaks up, they could easily fail to negotiate a deal. Operating in the dark, Peabody's bid to buy and Western's offer to sell might be so far apart that each party would be encouraged to withdraw. This situation is symptomatic of what negotiation scholars call the *negotiator's dilemma*. In this dilemma, both sides could create value if *both* were forthcoming with information about their needs and their business situations. But either will suffer if one shares its information and the other does not. Consider the possible outcomes shown in figure 6-1. Here it's clear that both companies will make modest gains if both are open and truthful. It's also clear that either party stands to make a major gain if it conceals information or misleads when the other is open and truthful.

In the negotiator's dilemma, a party puts itself at risk by being the first to disclose important information. It stands to benefit most by keeping its mouth shut and encouraging the other side to open up. If both sides maintain silence, however, both will be losers.

So how can this dilemma be resolved for mutual benefit? The

FIGURE 6-1

The Negotiator's Dilemma

		Western	
		Be open and truthful	Conceal or mislead
Peabody	Be open and truthful	Both companies make modest gains.	Small gain for Peabody; major gain for Western.
	Conceal or mislead	Major gain for Peabody; small gain for Western.	Neither company gains. Negotiations may fail.

Source: Adapted with permission from Michael D. Watkins, "Diagnosing and Overcoming Barriers to Agreement," Class Note 9-800-333 (Boston: Harvard Business School Publishing, revised May 8, 2000), 4.

best answer is cautious, mutual, and incremental information sharing. Here, one party takes a small risk: It reveals a small piece of information about its interests. It follows this revelation with a query:
"Now, tell us something about your interests." Reciprocity by the
other side helps create a climate of trust in which still further information can be safely shared. As trust and sharing continue, each party
puts more of its key cards on the table, and opportunities for mutual
value creating and value claiming are identified.

Structural Impediments

In some cases, the road to agreement is blocked by structural impediments. Here are a few typical examples:

- Not all the right parties are at the table. For example, a work
  schedule for developing a new product is being negotiated.
  The people from research and development and marketing
  are there, but no one invited the manufacturing people whose
  input is critical.

  Remedy: Get the right people on board.

- Other parties to the negotiation don't belong there—worse,
  they are getting in the way.

Remedy: Get the group to confront the individual or individuals who are blocking progress and ask them to step aside. If a person resists, appeal to a higher authority.

- One or more of the parties who legitimately belongs at the table is deliberately blocking progress toward an agreement.

  Remedy: If you have the organizational clout to prevail, tell this person or persons to back off. If you lack that clout, form a coalition of people at the table to deliver the same message.

- No one feels under any time pressure, and so negotiations drag on and on.

  Remedy: Avoid this by adding what Michael Watkins has called an action-forcing event, such as a deadline or progress meeting. For example, "We are giving your company an exclusive opportunity to bid on this work. However, if we cannot reach a mutually satisfactory agreement by March 15, then we will have to seek other bids." If a time component was not part of ongoing negotiations, consider adding one. "Since we are in agreement that things are moving too slowly, I suggest that we adopt a timeline that provides for completion of our negotiations by March 15."

- Agreement on this deal is predicated on agreement in another separate negotiation, which is going nowhere.

  Remedy: If it makes sense or is feasible, decouple the different deals. If that is not possible, consider adding a time constraint to the other deal.

Spoilers

Particularly in multiparty negotiations, certain stakeholders may prefer "no deal" as the outcome. Call them spoilers. They may have the power to block or sabotage your negotiations. These spoilers may have seats at the table, or they may not. For example, the president of the United States may negotiate a trade deal with a foreign nation, but two or three powerful senators who view the deal as contrary to the interests of their constituents may block ratification in Congress. An influential executive who has the ear of key board members can sometimes accomplish the same result.

You can anticipate this barrier to an agreement by identifying all key stakeholders, their respective interests, and the power of each to affect the agreement and its implementation. Then identify potential spoilers and consider the necessity of sweetening the deal in a way that would neutralize their incentive to sabotage an agreement.

Tips for Dealing with Spoilers

Many internal negotiations aim to create change within the organization. Change is a necessary condition of vitality, but it often creates winners and losers. And those who see themselves as potential losers do what they can to resist or undermine change.

"The reformer has enemies in all those who profit by the old order," Machiavelli warned his readers. And what held true in sixteenth-century Italy remains true today. Some people clearly enjoy advantages that—rightly or wrongly—they view as threatened by change. They may perceive change as a threat to their livelihoods, their perks, their workplace social arrangements, or their status in the organization.

Anytime people perceive themselves as losers in the outcome of a negotiation, expect resistance and possible sabotage. Resistance may be passive, in the form of noncommitment to the goals and the process for reaching them, or active, in the form of direct opposition or subversion. Here are some tips for dealing with resistance and possible sabotage:

• Always try to answer the question, "Where and how will this change create pain or loss in the organization?"

• Identify people who have something to lose, and try to anticipate how they will respond.

- Communicate the "why" of change to potential resisters. Explain the urgency of moving away from established routines or arrangements.

- Emphasize the benefits of change to potential resisters. Those benefits might be greater future job security, higher pay, and so forth. There's no guarantee that the benefits of change will exceed the losses to these individuals. However, explaining the benefits will help shift their focus from negatives to positives.

- Help resisters find new roles—roles that represent genuine contributions *and* mitigate their losses.

- Remember that some people resist change because it represents a loss of control over their daily lives. You can return some of that control by making them active partners in your change program.

- Build a coalition with sufficient strength to overpower the spoilers.

Differences in Gender and Culture

Our language, thought processes, perceptions, communication styles, and personalities are formed by a thicket of culture, gender, and social dynamics. Culture is a cluster of tendencies that are more prevalent in one group than another—how people behave and think. We tend to attribute any mystifying behavior in other people to, say, the French national character, the ways of women, the personality of lawyers, or even to the culture of a certain company.

But culture does not determine or predict any single individual's behaviors or choices: There are always great variations within given populations. Thus, an Italian engineer may have more in common with a German engineer than with an Italian artist. A female lawyer may have more in common with a male lawyer than with a female musician.

People often attribute a breakdown or difficulty in negotiation to gender or cultural differences, when these may not be the cause of the problem. They throw up their hands and say, "The problem is that she's a woman and can't deal with conflict." Or, "He's late because that's how Argentinians are with time." Don't make these mistakes. By attributing problems to gender or culture, you may miss the fact that the female negotiator is signaling her company's resistance point. Or you may fail to pick up on production problems at the Argentinian company.

If you are negotiating with someone from a culture very different from your own, and if you are experiencing problems understanding or dealing with each other, look for a pattern in these problems and ask: What kinds of issues are always tripping us up? What types of misunderstandings are we having? If you find a pattern, analyze it together.

If you have the time, review any available literature about the other negotiator's culture and how it compares with yours. How is it different? Does this explain the pattern of problems you have had?

Different cultures sometimes bring different, unspoken assumptions to the negotiating table. These can create barriers to agreement. Michael Watkins refers to assumptions as "the deeper, often unspoken beliefs that infuse and underpin social systems. These beliefs are the air that everyone breathes but never sees."[3] Look in particular at assumptions about who should make decisions, what is of value, and what will happen if agreement is reached.

Differences in organizational culture may also be behind the problems that plague negotiators. For example, if your meetings with a joint venture partner seem to be going nowhere, the difference between your organizational culture and that of the other party may be the problem. This is especially true when one company is highly entrepreneurial ("let's get this done) and the other is highly bureaucratic ("we must follow established procedures"). This was the problem with an R&D alliance between Alza, a small, entrepreneurial start-up based in California, and Ciba-Geigy, the giant Swiss pharmaceutical firm. As described by Gary Hamel and Yves Doz:

[Alza's founder] believed deeply in the value of an informal, egalitarian environment in which unique talents could bloom through self-structuring teams. Alza's teams worked quickly and informally to integrate the many technologies needed to develop advanced trans-dermal drug delivery systems. Ciba-Geigy, on the other hand, was a two-hundred-year-old company. . . . It was the epitome of a traditional, disciplined, dedicated European company. And as a large multinational company, Ciba-Geigy was formally structured and bureaucratic.[4]

As described by Hamel and Doz, deep historical, cultural, and organizational differences made collaboration and agreement between these companies very difficult. The Alza people expected their partner's people to work at a Silicon Valley pace, while Ciba's people wanted things to move more gradually. To make matters worse, the trust needed to bind the partnership together never developed. The Alza people were always fearful that their larger partner would usurp the one thing they had of value: their technology. This distrust resulted in collaboration along very narrow lines.

Difficulties in Communication

Communication is the medium of negotiation. You cannot make progress without it. Poor communication renders the simple treacherous and the difficult impossible. Communication problems cause deals to go sour and disputes to ripen. When you suspect that communication is causing the negotiation to go off track, try the following tactics:

- Ask for a break. Replay in your mind what has been communicated, how, and by whom. Look for a pattern. Does the confusion or misunderstanding arise from a single issue? Were important assumptions or expectations not articulated? After the break, raise the issue in a nonaccusatory way. Offer to listen while the other side explains its perspective on the issue. Listen actively, acknowledging their point of view. Explain your perspective. Then, try to pinpoint the problem.

- If the spokesperson of your negotiating team seems to infuriate the other side, have someone else act as spokesperson. Ask the other side to do the same if their spokesperson drives your people up the wall.

- Jointly document progress as it is made. This is particularly important in multiphase negotiations. It will solve the problem of someone saying, "I don't remember agreeing to that."

The Power of Dialogue

Dialogue is a powerful mode of communication and an effective antidote to most, if not all, of the human barriers identified in this chapter. It is a time-tested communication form in which parties exchange views and ideas with the goal of reaching amicable agreement. Dialogue is usually the very best way to peel back the layers of problems, bring undisclosed concerns to center stage, develop solutions, and reach common understandings.

Though the practice of dialogue between two or more individuals undoubtedly goes back into the mists of time, Plato, through his Socratic dialogues, helped the Western world appreciate its power. Plato's purpose was not to tell us what *he* thought directly, but to teach us how to toss ideas back and forth in a logical process that eventually leads to the truth and common understanding. That same logical process makes negotiations run more smoothly, draws out the best ideas, and builds agreement around them.

Dialogue can also help you give direction without telling people what to do in so many words—which is what managers in today's participatory organizations must learn to do. For such managers, negotiating with people is as important as directing them. For example, instead of saying, "Have the inventory report on my desk at 3 P.M. tomorrow," try something like this:

Manager: What progress have you made on the inventory report?

Employee: It's almost ready. I only have one section to complete.

Manager: Good. Do you see any problem in getting it all wrapped up by tomorrow afternoon?

Employee: No, not if you need it by then.

Manager: Yes, I do need it by 3 P.M. at the latest.

Employee: You can count on it.

What works between managers and their people can also work between negotiating parties if they start slowly, practice active listening, and gradually develop the level of trust that problem solving requires.

Summing Up

This chapter examined typical barriers to negotiated agreements and what you can do to overcome or eliminate them.

- Die-hard bargainers will pull for every advantage and try to make every concession come from you. You can deal with these people if you understand the game they are playing, withhold useful information from them (they'll only use it against you) unless they demonstrate a willingness to reciprocate, and make it clear that you don't mind walking away. If you don't want to walk away—or cannot—do whatever you can to strengthen your position and your alternative to a deal.

- Lack of trust is a serious impediment to making a deal. Nevertheless, agreements are possible if you take precautions, require enforcement mechanisms, build incentives for compliance into the deal, and insist on compliance transparency.

- It's difficult to make a deal—and impossible to create value—in the absence of information. What are the other side's interests?

What does it have to offer? What is it willing to trade? Ironically, fear of advantaging the other side encourages parties to withhold the information needed to create value for both sides. Each is reluctant to be the first to open up. This is the negotiator's dilemma. The solution to this dilemma is cautious, mutual, and incremental information sharing.

- Structural impediments include the absence of important parties at the table, the presence of others who don't belong there but get in the way, and lack of pressure to move toward an agreement. Remedies to these impediments were provided.

- Spoilers are people who block or undermine negotiations. Several tips were offered for neutralizing or winning over these individuals, including the creation of winning coalitions.

- Cultural and gender difference can be barriers to agreement, particularly when one of the parties brings to the table a set of assumptions that the other side fails to notice: assumptions about who will make key decisions, what is of value, and what will happen if agreement is reached. Negotiators who represent organizations with conflicting cultures (e.g., entrepreneurial versus bureaucratic) are also likely to experience problems in reaching agreements.

- Communication problems can also create barriers. You can diffuse them by insisting that each team be led by an effective communicator and by practicing active listening, documenting progress as it is made, and establishing real dialogue between parties.

- Dialogue can eliminate or lower all of the barriers described in this chapter.

7

Mental Errors

How to Recognize and Avoid Them

Key Topics Covered in This Chapter

- *Escalation*

- *Partisan perceptions*

- *Irrational expectations*

- *Overconfidence*

- *Unchecked emotions*

THE PREVIOUS CHAPTER described the kinds of structural problems that separate willing parties from negotiated agreements. This chapter describes the mental errors that parties commit during the negotiating process. Each of these errors represents a case of shooting oneself in the foot, and each is amenable to self-correction.

Escalation

In their book *Negotiating Rationally*, Max Bazerman and Margaret Neale point to "irrational escalation" as an error committed by otherwise level-headed businesspeople when they get into difficult and competitive negotiations. In their definition, *irrational escalation* is "continuing a previously selected course of action beyond what rational analysis would recommend."[1] It might also be called "overcommitment." Bazerman and Neale cite the example of Robert Campeau's ill-fated 1987 acquisition of Federated Department Stores, parent company of Bloomingdale's, as a case of irrational escalation. Campeau, who wanted Bloomingdale's both for its inherent earning power and its potential to anchor various shopping malls he planned to develop, pursued his quarry boldly despite strong competition from Macy's. This rival also wanted the company and put in a high bid. Not to be outdone, Campeau bid some $500 million above Macy's last offer. With that bold stroke, he won the contest—but he also plunged his own organization into bankruptcy.

The lesson of the Bloomingdale's story, as Bazerman and Neale artfully point out, is that even a good strategy will produce a bad result if it is escalated beyond a point where it no longer makes sense. Bloomingdale's was a great prize, but not at the price Campeau paid. Paying too much is a lesson found repeated over and over in the annals of business.

Why do normally shrewd businesspeople fall into the escalation error? Here are possible reasons—and possible remedies.

1. Their egos cannot abide "losing." CEOs and other senior executives are accustomed to getting what they want. And they don't want to be seen coming home empty-handed from a negotiation, particularly when it's highly visible. So, when winning requires paying more than every rational measure says is smart, their egos tempt them to pay. They then point to "future synergies" or other nebulous values as justification for their behavior.

2. Auctions and other bidding contests that pit individuals against each other encourage irrational behavior. As one consultant put it, "Collectors in particular do not exhibit rational price behavior."[2] In the absence of any particular price expectations, they are more likely to bid up to a price they can afford than to a price they know something to be worth. The urge to have something—and to win out over other bidders—overcomes their business sense.

3. A principal/agent problem is at work. In general, the businesspeople who spend to win beyond the point of rationality do so with OPM (other people's money). As *agents* of the shareholders (the true principals), they can take credit for the "win" and charge the costs to the real owners of the business. It's unlikely that agents would be so bold, or so reckless, if they were spending their own hard-earned savings.

Remedies

- Get a firm handle on your alternatives to the deal *before* you negotiate. Remind yourself that money you don't throw away on an overpriced deal is money you'll have available to invest in

those alternatives. Remember, too, that the money your com-
petitor is using to defeat you is money it won't have at its disposal when the next deal comes down the pike.

- Prior to negotiations, be very objective and empirical in setting a
price beyond which good sense dictates walking away. Seek agreement and mutual support within your team regarding that price.
"Then we are agreed that we will not offer more than $350,000?
Does anyone have a different view?" Agreement by many people
regarding a price will reduce the temptation to escalate.

- Set clear breakpoints where you and your team will stop and
take stock of where you are in the negotiations and where you
are headed.

- If during negotiations new information suggests raising the
walk-away price, apply objectivity in recalculating that walk-
away price.

- With respect to the principal/agent problem, the best solution
is to align the negotiator's rewards with the economic interests
of shareholders. (This topic is discussed further in chapter 9.)
The board of directors should also be diligent in safeguarding
the interests of shareholders against irrational behavior on the
part of the CEO. This is a tough problem because most board
members are members of the same fraternity as the CEO; in
the United States, for example, the majority of corporation
board members are also CEOs—that is, agents of shareholders.

Partisan Perceptions

A *partisan perception* is a psychological phenomenon that causes
people to perceive the world with a bias in their own favor or toward
their own point of view. For example, loyal fans of either team in a
sporting event perceive that the referee was unfair to their side. Dem-
ocrats and Republicans watching the same presidential debate perceive that their candidate "won." A panel of engineers representing

two joint venture partners fails to reach a conclusion as to how well one of the companies has performed its part of an agreement.

Effective negotiators know how to stand outside a situation and see it objectively, thus avoiding partisan perceptions. They can also get inside the minds of the other parties and see their unique—and partisan—viewpoints. You can do the same if you try the following:

- Recognize partisan perception as a phenomenon to which we all fall prey.

- Put yourself in the other side's position. How would the issue look to you then?

- Pose the issue to colleagues (without revealing which side you are on) and solicit their opinions.

To convey your position to the other party:

- Try to pose the problem as it appears to you, and ask how they view it.

- Use an analogy or a hypothetical situation to frame the problem as you see it.

Another technique for reducing partisan perceptions is for the opposing sides to reverse their roles, as in the following example:

When two city councilors proposed expanding the town's existing golf course, local environmentalists and outdoors enthusiasts objected. "An expanded municipal course will provide substantial revenue for the town," argued the two councilors. "Not true," said their opponents. "It makes no economic sense, and you'd have to gut our last remaining woodland to build it."

Faced with a divided community, the mayor formed a fact-finding committee to investigate and report on the various merits and demerits of the golf course expansion, with all interested parties represented. Each side presented its facts—on the economics of the expansion, on environmental impacts, on community values, and so forth. But neither side would accept the other's facts or interpretations. And each side impugned the other side's honesty.

To help bring the committee members to a point where they could develop an objective report, the mayor asked the opposing sides to reverse roles. Thus, the environmentalists would represent the "facts" gathered by those who advocated golf course expansion, and vice versa. Each was asked to develop a coherent and compelling case using the facts of their opponent.

By the end of the role reversal exercise, each side had a greater appreciation for the other's point of view. And though they continued to disagree on key points, they were able to develop a report for the mayor and the community that fairly represented all information and viewpoints.

If any of these suggestions fail, bring in a neutral third party or expert to provide unbiased guidance.

Irrational Expectations

Agreement is hard to find when one or more parties have expectations that cannot be fulfilled. This eliminates any zone of possible agreement. Many people commit this mental error as they enter into negotiations. Consider this example:

Like every other budding author, Marie had read stories about the fabulous royalty advances that some authors received for their manuscripts—and even their proposed manuscripts. "The pope got $4 million," she told a friend. "Hillary got $8 million!" She didn't expect to get nearly that much for her self-help book, The Joy of Antique Hunting. *After all, it was her first work. But she did expect around $100,000.*

Unfortunately, the publisher Marie approached with her ten-page proposal did not see it her way. "I'm sorry, but $10,000 is the most we're willing to pay," she was told.

"You've got to be kidding," she exploded. "That's not even enough to cover the three or four months I'd have to take from work to write the book!"

After some harsh words with the editor, Marie moved on to another publisher, where (guess what?) she got the same reaction to her

demand for a large advance. "You people don't even understand your
own business!" she fumed.

"Look, Marie," editor number two counseled. "You're a first-time
author with no track record. And your subject will appeal only to a nar-
row niche of readers. It's not the stuff from which best-sellers are made
by a long shot." The words weren't even out of his mouth when he
heard Marie slam her phone down on the receiver.

After two more such disappointing encounters, Marie's best friend
offered some advice. "Marie, you've now had encouraging conversations
with several mainstream publishers. All have liked your proposal, but
none have been willing to give you anything near the advance you in-
sist on having. This might be the best you can expect with this type of
book. Your expectations may be out of line."

"Baloney!" she huffed. "They're just trying to take advantage
of me."

Indeed, Marie's expectations were out of line with reality as each of
the publishers saw it. Nor did she have the bargaining power to force
them to accept her point of view. Were it not for this irrational expectation, she might have been successful in negotiating an agreement with any one of the four publishers.

Cases like this one are not uncommon, but they are not insoluble.
In Marie's case, her irrational expectation resulted in no ZOPA, as described in chapter 2. With the publisher's reservation price somewhere around $10,000 and Marie's somewhere around $100,000,
there was simply no overlap in which agreement could be struck. This
sorry situation might have been remedied if the parties had provided
one or both of the following:

- **Educating dialogue.** The editor might have had a calm, heart-
  to-heart conversation with Marie in which he indicated the
  number of copies he'd have to sell to cover Marie's $100,000
  royalty advance. He could also have indicated the unit sales of
  comparable books, none of which sold enough copies to earn
  the level of advance Marie expected. For example: "Look,
  Marie, in order for your book to earn $100,000 in royalties,
  we'd have to sell at least 50,000 copies, and we believe that that

number of sales is highly unlikely. We have published three books on antique collecting over the past several years, and not one of them surpassed 12,000 copies. Would you like to see the sales figures for yourself?" This bit of education might have induced Marie to reduce her reservation price substantially.

- **New information.** Marie might have provided information (if she had it) to encourage the editor to increase his reservation price—and his expectation of future sales. For example: "Here's a letter I recently received from the marketing director of *Antiquing Monthly*, which has 200,000 subscribers. He indicates his interest in purchasing 10,000 copies to use as a new subscriber premium."

Either of these tactics would have defused the problem caused by irrational expectations.

What are your expectations as you prepare to negotiate with your boss, your customer, or your direct reports? Are they realistic? Will the other side have similar expectations on key negotiating points? These could be deal busters if your expectations and theirs are significantly at variance. If they are, you must bring expectations in line with fact-based reality.

Overconfidence

Confidence is a good thing. It gives us the courage we need to tackle difficult and uncertain ventures—such as negotiations. Too much confidence, however, can set a person up for a fall. Overconfidence encourages us to overestimate our own strengths and underestimate those of our rivals. Consider the example of the American Civil War. Each side expected to whip the other quickly and "have the boys home" within a few weeks. Four years and hundreds of thousands of casualties later, the contending sides were still slugging it out—and on a scale that neither side could have envisioned. As evidence that this mental error is not exclusive to Americans, we have the example of the Imperial Japanese Navy on the eve of the Battle of Midway. Its planners dismissed the U.S. Navy as incompetent and unwilling to fight. That overconfidence encouraged them to take a tactical risk that resulted in heavy losses and a turning of the tide in the Pacific.

We observe similar overconfidence in business and interpersonal disputes, where one or both parties reject settlement in favor of litigation. "We are very confident that the court will find in our favor. The lawyers say that we have a very strong case."

Overconfidence can blindside you to dangers and opportunities. It is reinforced by a related mental error known as *groupthink*. The late Irving Janus, the Yale psychologist who coined the term, defined groupthink as "a mode of thinking that people engage in when they are deeply involved in a cohesive ingroup, when the members' strivings for unanimity override their motivation to realistically appraise alternative courses of action."[3] Groupthink is the result of convergence of thinking around a norm. Unfortunately, that convergence is driven less by objectivity than by social psychological pressures. In the end, opposing views are repressed in favor of homogeneity and an illusion of certitude. Those who "think otherwise" are either reeducated or pushed out. Here are some symptoms of groupthink:

- An illusion of invulnerability exists.

- Leaders are insulated (protected) from contradictory evidence.

- Members accept confirming data only.

- Those holding divergent views are censured.

- Alternatives are not considered.

- Members of the "out" group are discounted or demonized.

Do you see any of these symptoms in your negotiating team? If you do, here is a suggestion for getting rid of them before groupthink leads to critical thinking errors: Empower a team of bright and respected people to find and objectively represent the relevant data. This same team should examine and report back on every one of your key assumptions.

Uucouftatted

Unchecked Emotions

People tend to assume that unchecked emotions occur in divorce and other personal negotiations, but rarely in business. Not so. Business partnership dissolutions are called business "divorces" for a very good reason: They involve tremendous anger and personal vitriol.

Bad things happen when anger takes control of a negotiation. The parties stop focusing on logic and rational self-interest. Inflicting damage on the other side becomes the goal, even when doing so causes damage to one's own interests. Consider this example:

> *Harold and Simon were joint owners of a small corporation. Each held an equal share. Harold was eager to withdraw from the business and pursue other interests. He also wanted his son, Alex, to step in to fill his shoes, and planned to gradually sell his ownership shares to Alex.*
>
> *"No way," insisted Simon. "Alex is totally inept, and I won't have him around here wrecking everything I've built over the years."*
>
> *"What do you mean 'everything you've built,' Simon? This company has grown because of my leadership, and I want my son to have an opportunity to learn the business and build his own legacy."*
>
> *"Over my dead body. Either you sell your shares to me, or I'll torpedo this business."*

Sounds like a nasty divorce, doesn't it? Huge damage is caused when negotiators allow their emotions to get out of control. This is often observed in cases of closely held family businesses when the founder/patriarch tries to retire and turn the reins over to a hand-picked successor. In some cases, siblings turn on each other and their parents and practically destroy the business through interpersonal warfare and expensive lawsuits.

If you see this happening in your negotiations, try the following:

- Agree to a cooling-off period and tell the combatants to go to their separate corners.

- Enlist an objective moderator. A moderator who has the best interests of the contending parties at heart may be successful in dampening emotions, acting as a medium of communication,

Fairness Matters

Anger and irrational behavior are often triggered by an offense to one party's sense of fairness. People will sometimes forego tangible personal gains rather than be party to an agreement that treats them unfairly. Consider how most people would behave in the following situation, which we've adapted from a story told in Bazerman and Neale.[4]

Stephanie and George are having lunch in the company cafeteria. Their boss sits down and says, "I have $100 in my pocket, which I'm willing to give to you. There are only two conditions." Looking at George and showing him a stack of $1 bills, he says, "The first condition is that George must decide how the $100 will be split between you. The second condition is that I will keep the money if you two cannot agree on how the money will be divided."

Stephanie and George are both amazed by the offer, but not entirely surprised, since their boss is always pulling stunts like this. George thinks to himself that any amount he allocates to Stephanie is money she would not have otherwise. Rationally, she should be willing to agree to any split he offers. "Okay," he says. "Here's the deal. I'll give Stephanie $20 and keep $80 for myself."

"Keep your lousy $20," Stephanie says, leaving the table. "That's really unfair."

The boss laughs and returns the wad of bills to his pocket, leaving George empty-handed.

The lesson of this little story is that rationality can be trumped by one party's offended sense of fairness. George wrongly assumed that Stephanie's rationality would get her to accept the $20/$80 split.

and providing the "adult supervision" necessary during subsequent negotiations.

In the absence of a moderator, do the following:

- Determine what is making the other negotiator angry. What does this deal or this dispute mean to him? Listen very carefully when he gets angry. Search for clues.

- Respond to what appears to be the emotional problem. Express empathy for what this means to her.

- Remember that people are most often angered and frustrated at a personal level by perceived deception, unfairness, humiliation, or loss of pride and lack of respect. You can avoid these land mines by focusing discussion on the issues and the problems instead of on individuals and their personalities.

If none of these suggestions work, you might call for a break in the negotiations or try to make arrangements to work with a negotiator who is less emotional, if that is possible. Otherwise, suggest that the negotiations proceed with a neutral, third-party facilitator.

Summing Up

Mental errors by negotiators can result in no deal or a bad deal. This chapter has examined five common mental errors.

- Escalation—that is, irrational escalation—is the continuation of a previously selected course of action beyond the point where it continues to makes sense. Some people commit this error because they cannot stand losing. Others fall prey to auction fever.

- Partisan perception is the psychological phenomenon that causes people to perceive truth with a built-in bias in their own favor or toward their own point of view.

- Irrational expectations are an error insofar as they eliminate zones of possible agreement.

- Overconfidence in negotiating is dangerous. It encourages negotiators to overestimate their strengths and underestimate their rivals. It is reinforced by groupthink, a mode of thinking driven by consensus that tends to override the motivation to realistically appraise alternative courses of action. The antidote to both overconfidence and groupthink is to have one or more objective outsiders examine one's assumptions.

- Unchecked emotions are frequently observed in business negotiations, and generally result in self-injury. Among the remedies recommended in the chapter are a cooling-off period and the use of an objective moderator.

8

When Relationships Matter

A Different Notion of Winning

Key Topics Covered in This Chapter

- *Why relationships matter*

- *How perceptions of relationship value affect negotiations*

- *Separating the deal from the broader relationship*

T HIS CHAPTER considers negotiating with employees, customers, and suppliers—parties who represent important relationships. Unlike many situations in which negotiators try to maximize outcomes in their favor, these are situations in which the relationship with the other side is of equal or greater importance, particularly over time. "Winning" in these cases, even if the negotiation appears purely distributive, means more than simply claiming the most value.

Why Relationships Matter

People tend to think of negotiating as something that takes place between arm's-length entities trying to cut the best possible deal for themselves without regard to the future: a car salesperson and potential customer, a plaintiff and defendant in a product liability case, divorcing spouses, and so forth. Although this impression is valid in many cases, other negotiations take place between individuals and entities that do not deal at arm's length or in transactional ways. These parties have important relationships and for one reason or another hope to retain them. These include managers and their direct reports, manufacturers and their key suppliers, and individual employees who are trying to get things done through collaboration with others.

Two phenomena of the past twenty years or so account for the frequency of negotiations in which relationships matter. The first is the flattening of organizations. Flatter organizations and wider spans of management control have dispersed power, giving lower-level managers and employees greater autonomy for action and decision making. With power thus dispersed, negotiation has replaced "you will do this" with "here's what needs to be done" as a means of focusing resources and getting work accomplished. This results in negotiated solutions between parties who need to maintain strong relationships.

The change *within* organizations is paralleled by changes *between* them. Companies are less inclined to pit one supplier against another to extract the best deal. Instead of squeezing their suppliers, many leading companies are viewing them as long-term partners. At the same time, companies have entered into many more joint ventures and strategic alliances—deals in which relationships must be managed with care.

Harvard professor John Kotter underscores the importance of relationships and their features:

> *Good working relationships based on some combination of respect, admiration, perceived need, obligation, and friendship are a critical source of power in helping to get things done. Without these relationships, even the best possible idea could be rejected or resisted in an environment where diversity breeds suspicion and interdependence precludes giving orders to most of the relevant players.*[1]

The importance of good relationships changes how people deal with each other when they negotiate. It moderates extreme value-claiming behavior. Why? There are three reasons:

1. **Future transactions of real value are anticipated:** Being too greedy today would risk losing those valuable transactions.

2. **Reciprocity by the other side is expected:** You give a little in this transaction in the expectation that the other party will help you later.

3. **A good relationship engenders trust:** Trust reduces the cost of monitoring compliance and nitpicking adherence to the terms of an agreement.

How Perceptions of Relationship Value Affect Negotiations

Obviously, negotiations between parties who value their relationship will be different from those between parties who place no value on the relationship. Consider these examples:

> *After three years of constant disagreement and bickering over how to run their make-to-order dress shop, Phyllis and Sharon are breaking up their business partnership. Each blames the other for the split, and each is too bitter to speak with the other about how they should allocate responsibility for the shop's assets and liabilities.*

> *Acme Sound Corporation and one of its first-tier parts suppliers, Waltham Widgets, are negotiating a dispute involving a particular lot of 1,000 transistors. "We've experienced a high level of warranty claims on amplifiers that incorporated those parts," says Acme's purchasing manager. "Our analysis points to Waltham's transistors as the root cause, and we've suffered financial losses owing to warranty claims and damages to our reputation for quality stereo equipment." Waltham's representative doesn't see it that way. Nevertheless, the two parties are working to resolve their differences in ways that will not impinge on their ability to continue their business relationship.*

The disputants in each of these examples have relationships, but they treat them in starkly different manners. Phyllis and Sharon are negotiating as if their relationship has no future value—which appears to be the case. Each will attempt to claim as large a share of the remains of the business as possible. Claiming value is, in fact, the prime objective of each side.

Acme Sound and Waltham Widgets likewise have a relationship, one that each values. As a manufacturer, Acme knows from experience that a new and untested supplier can jeopardize its operations. In its view, finding reliable suppliers and learning to work with them is the best way to stabilize its production. Waltham Widgets has a similar opinion. As a result, each is willing to temper its desire for total victory in the dispute. "Waltham has been an important partner in our growth over the past twelve years, and this is our first real problem with them," says Acme's purchasing manager. "But quality is so important in our industry that any lapse must be dealt with immediately and directly. We have to juggle these two facts."

Waltham's representative voices a similar line: "Acme is an important customer, and our people work closely with it in everything from new product design to just-in-time delivery. We don't believe that our transistors were the source of their problems, and we want to work with them to prove it—and to find where the problem actually occurred."

The value to be claimed in both examples can be envisioned as a fixed pie, as shown in figure 8-1. Phyllis and Sharon see that pie as 100 percent monetary value, and each is trying to claim as large a piece as possible. As far as they are concerned, there is no relationship value. The stereo company and its supplier, however, recognize that both monetary and relationship values are at stake. And each knows that being too aggressive in claiming monetary value will reduce the relationship value.

Now, here's one important complication: Although both Acme and Waltham recognize relationship value as part of the negotiation dynamics, it's very likely that neither party sees it to quite the same

FIGURE 8-1

Monetary and Relationship Values

Phyllis vs. Sharon

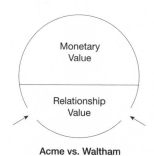

Acme vs. Waltham

degree. One will most certainly value the relationship more highly than the other. It's also very likely that the following are true:

1. Neither side can quantify its view of relationship value. In fact, the assessment of value is likely to vary among individuals within the same company. For example, the Acme purchasing manager may have very different perspectives on the Waltham relationship than the Acme financial officer. The financial officer will be more interested in monetary measures. The purchasing manager will also be concerned with dollars and cents, but she will also place a value on the supplier's delivery reliability, defect rate, and ability to quickly scale up production in response to customer demand.

2. Neither side can know how the other assesses the relationship value. For example, Acme's purchasing manager may have her own thoughts about the relationship value, but she cannot know with any certainty how Waltham, as a company, values its relationship with Acme. "Do they value our relationship so highly that they'll cave in on our demand for monetary damages?" she wonders.

These two forms of uncertainty will affect the tactics and intensity of how each side negotiates with the other.

Now consider the negotiations in which you are presently engaged, and try to answer these questions:

- **How greatly should relationship value influence my negotiating goals and tactics?** Your answer should be framed by two considerations: (1) the extent to which you will deal with the other side in the future, and (2) a rough calculation of the present value of benefits you anticipate receiving through future dealings with this party. Obviously, if you are unlikely to deal with this party again, there will be no relationship value to worry about. Value claiming should be your goal. But if the opposite is the case, you need to make a mental tally of the future benefits, and develop a strategy for value creating and sharing between both parties.

- **To what extent does relationship value matter to the party with whom I'm dealing?** If you can answer this, you'll know how far you can push in claiming value for yourself. In determining the answer, put yourself in the shoes of the other party and apply the two framing considerations discussed earlier: the likelihood of future dealings with the other side, and an estimate of anticipated future benefits from those dealings.

Doing It Right

Negotiating expert Danny Ertel underscores the problems associated with negotiations in which elements of the deal and the relationship are intertwined:

> [Negotiators] fear that if they push too hard to get the best deal possible today, they may jeopardize their company's ability to do business with the other party in the future. Or they fear that if they pay too much attention to the relationship, they'll end up giving away too much and make a lousy deal. Though natural, such confusion is dangerous. It leaves the negotiator open to manipulation by the other party.[2]

The danger of manipulation is obviously greatest when one party values the relationship and the other does not. Ertel gives the example of an accounting firm that must annually renew its auditing contract with a major client company. The client is interested in cutting a lower-priced deal, while the accounting firm is interested in a long-term relationship. So when the client demands a lower price, the accounting firm capitulates for the sake of the relationship. Several years of this, however, make the relationship profitless for the accounting firm.

Is this reminiscent of your negotiations? If it is, you might consider the actual value of your relationships with those particular customers. How profitable are they? "Over the years," writes Ertel, "I have asked hundreds of executives to reflect on their business relationships and to ask themselves what kind of customer they make more concessions to, do more costly favors for, and generally give away more value to."[3] Their usual response, he reports, is that concessions are made to the most difficult and least valuable customers—and always in the vain hope that the relationship will improve!

How can you avoid falling into this same trap? Ertel's advice is to distinguish between the deal and the relationship—that is, to draw a clear distinction between the components of the deal and the components of the relationship. It may help to create a list like the one in table 8-1, where one column itemizes all the deal issues and the other does the same for relationship issues.

Don't look at the negotiation as a seesaw in which improving the relationship must result in a loss in the deal itself. Instead, they should rise or fall in tandem. According to Ertel,

> A strong relationship creates trust, which allows the parties to share information more freely, which in turn leads to more creative and valuable agreements and to a greater willingness to continue working together. But when a deal is struck that is not very attractive to one or both parties, chances are that they will invest less time and effort in working together, they will become more wary in communicating with each other, and their relationship will grow strained.[4]

TABLE 8-1

Categorizing the Issues in a Negotiation

Deal Issues	Relationship Issues
Price at different volume break points	Recognition of mutual long-term goals
Service agreements	Recognition of individual goals and interests
Replacement of obsolete equipment	Future opportunities for collaboration
Disputed resolutions	Continued trust and respect
Termination terms	
Assignment of the vendor's responsibilities under the contract	

Source: Adapted with permission from Danny Ertel, "Turning Negotiation into a Corporate Capability," *Harvard Business Review,* May–June 1999, 62.

Figure 8-2 illustrates Ertel's view of the deal-relationship cycle. In the "usual way," exploitation of the deal by one party creates a vicious circle of distrust and a withholding of information. Both the deal and the relationship eventually suffer. A zero-sum mentality eventually prevails. In the "better approach," negotiators do not feel compelled to trade a good relationship for a good deal. As a result, they trade information and creative ideas more freely, expanding the possibilities of the deal. This leads to a virtuous circle of improved trust and deals that satisfy the core interests of all parties.

FIGURE 8-2

The Deal-Relationship Cycle

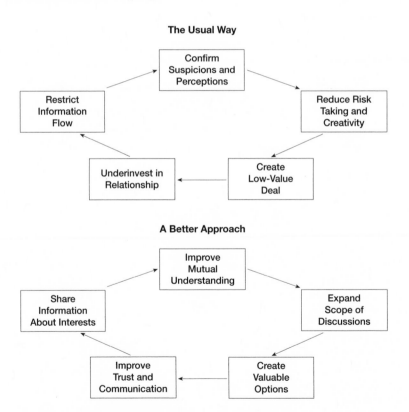

Source: Adapted with permission from Danny Ertel, "Turning Negotiation into a Corporate Capability," *Harvard Business Review*, May–June 1999, 64.

If relationships rank high among your organization's strategic goals, be forewarned that you could pay a personal price in pursuing them. Why? Because many companies still talk out of both sides of their mouths. On the one hand, they say that long-term relationships matter. On the other hand, they generally reward negotiators for delivering on monetary or other measurable values: the most advantageous settlement, the lowest-cost supplier contract, the most favorable contract terms, and so forth. We'll talk more about this problem—and its remedies—later in this book.

Tips on Managing Relationship Value

If you want to keep a relationship on an even keel, manage it as you would any other activity that matters to you.

- **Create trust.** Trust is created when people see tangible evidence that one's words and actions are in harmony. So avoid making commitments you may be unable to honor, and always do what you have committed to do. Trust is also created when you acknowledge and demonstrate respect for the other party's core interests.

- **Communicate.** The different parties should communicate their interests, their capabilities, and their concerns to each other. For example, if you agreed to complete a customer survey for the marketing vice president within thirty days but have hit a logjam, communicate that information to him.

- **Never sweep mistakes under the rug.** Mistakes are bound to happen. Acknowledging and addressing them—quickly—is always the best course of action.

- **Ask for feedback.** If everything appears to be going as planned, never assume that the other side sees it the same way. Be proactive in uncovering problems. The other side will respect you for it. Ask questions such as these: "Is everything happening as you expected?" "Are the parts reaching your plant on schedule?" "Did my report cover all important points?"

not hierarchical

Summing Up

This chapter examined the relationship value that is part of so many of today's agreements, both between separate entities and between employees of the same organization.

- Flatter organizations and the desire of companies to build long-term links with suppliers are two important reasons why relationships matter in many of today's negotiations.

- Relationship value moderates extreme value-claiming behavior. Negotiating parties understand that trying too hard to claim value today will risk losing opportunities for claiming value in future transactions.

- Parties who perceive no relationship value will aggressively claim value.

- Even when both parties recognize a relationship value, there is likely to be an imbalance in how strongly each party feels about that value. This can lead to manipulation of the party to whom the relationship matters most.

- Negotiators must separate the deal from the broader relationship.

Negotiating for Others

Whose Interests Come First?

Key Topics Covered in This Chapter

- *Why people engage agents to represent them in negotiations*

- *The problems of informational asymmetries, divided interests, and conflicts of interest— and how to deal with them*

I N S O M E C A S E S , people and organizations represent their own interests. In many other cases, however, they are represented by others. These others may be independent agents contracted to represent one of the parties. They may be non-independent agents—that is, employees—charged with representing their companies. Or they may be officials of an organization, such as a labor union, whose responsibility is to represent the interests of their members. This chapter considers the role of these various agents and potential problems that arise from their use.

Independent Agents

An *agent* is a person charged with representing the interests of another (a principal) in negotiations with a third party. Many professionals—lawyers, accountants, brokers—enter into contracts to represent others. Consider the lawyer's role in a divorce settlement. We might describe the lawyer as an agent since he or she represents a client in return for a fee. Think of a typical lawyer in a divorce case. She has no involvement with the client except insofar as she has been engaged to represent the client in a highly defined manner: in drafting legal documents, drawing up positions, and negotiating a settlement with the other side—and possibly representing the client in court.

In theory, the lawyer in the divorce case must put her personal interests on the shelf and represent only those of the client. By both statute and custom, she has a fiduciary responsibility toward the client to do so. In practice, no human being is capable of acting as the perfect agent of another. The lawyer will have concerns about time and reputation that will inevitably influence what she does.

Generally, people hire an independent agent to represent them for either or both of the following reasons:

- **The agent has greater expertise.** Engaging the services of an agent is usually a good idea when the other side is more experienced, more knowledgeable, or a sharper bargainer than you. For example: Nineteen-year-old Billy can put a basketball through the hoop from anywhere on the court, but he doesn't know a thing about contracts or how much he might be able to get from a major basketball team. Recognizing his own shortcomings in this area, he hires an agent who has knowledge and experience in contract negotiations to represent him.

- **To put some distance between oneself and the other party.** Will you be bargaining with a friend or valued business associate? If you are, are you prepared to drive a hard bargain? Probably not—doing so could damage that important relationship. By engaging an agent, you can put some distance between yourself and the other side, thereby avoiding some (but not all) relationship complications. Consider the case of Veronica, a best-selling romance novelist. She is ready to negotiate a contract for her next book, *The Breathless Duchess.* To avoid straining her working relationship with her editor, Tony, she engages a literary agent to represent her in contract negotiations. Since the agent is not a friend of Tony, he'll have no reluctance in pressing for the largest royalty advance and the best possible deal for Veronica.

Non-Independent Agents

Some individuals act as non-independent agent representatives in negotiations. A purchasing manager negotiates regularly with suppliers on behalf of his employer. He acts as the employer's agent but, unlike the lawyer described earlier, is part of the organization on whose behalf he is negotiating. The same can be said of the union representative seated at the collective bargaining table, and of the corporate

advertising manager whose job is to select an ad agency and negotiate terms of payment and the timing of delivery.

Agency Issues

Regardless of whether the agent is independent or a member of
one's organization, the decision to be represented by another poses
some big challenges. These flow from information asymmetries, divided interests among the principals, and conflicts of interest.

Information Asymmetries

Information asymmetry simply means that one party has more information than the other. This can be a problem. If the principal has
more information than the agent, then the agent may not know how
best to represent the principal. More often, however, the agent—
whether independent or non-independent—possesses the greater
share of information. Some of this information flows from the agent's
superior expertise; other critical information is often picked up at
the negotiating table itself. The agent's greater information can create a problem of trust between the principal and the agent.

Consider this example:

> *Fred is the purchasing manager for Gonzo Furniture, a maker of office
> furniture and work cubicles. He and Jane, the company's manufacturing
> manager, have been delegated to negotiate with As You Like It, Inc., a
> specialized supplier of materials to the furniture industry. The two com-
> panies have not done business before.*
>
> *Gonzo's strategy in dealing with suppliers has been to extract the
> lowest price and the best conditions, often pitting one supplier against an-
> other. The senior management team has grown up on that approach. Fred
> and Jane, however, are beginning to question that low-price practice. As You
> Like It has demonstrated its ability to provide just-in-time delivery and
> preassembly of key components. It is also capable of assuming responsibil-
> ity for other material requirements as a "tier 1" supplier, in effect giving
> Gonzo an opportunity to outsource some activities that add no value.*

Fred and Jane like what they've heard, and their phone calls to clients of As You Like It assure them that the company can deliver on its promises. "A deal with As You Like It would help us modernize our supply chain operations," says Jane, "and give us a real opportunity to move into fast, mass-customized production." Fred agrees, adding that the deal would reduce materials inventories and their associated costs. "We'll pay more to do business with this supplier, but we'll be gaining real advantages in manufacturing and more rapid customer delivery."

In this example, Fred and Jane have gathered some very important information in their negotiating sessions with As You Like It representatives. That information has opened their minds to opportunities to improve their approach to manufacturing and has given them insight that would make it possible to move beyond win-lose negotiations to something capable of creating greater value. The company's decision makers, however, are not privy to this information and its nuances. All they know is that doing business with this new supplier will cost them more money. "I'm starting to wonder if Fred and Jane know what they're doing," says the CEO. The information asymmetry has separated the principals from their agents, creating a gap of distrust.

How can principals and their agents avoid the problems caused by information asymmetries? Here are some suggestions:

- To the greatest extent possible, principals should give agents information about interests—what they care about.

- Agents should regularly communicate information gathered at the negotiating table. That information should be discussed, and the agent should ask, "In light of this new information, how should I proceed?"

Divided Interests

Many agents face the challenge of serving divided internal interests. Not every organization—be it a union, a company, or an operating unit—is of one mind as to its core interests. This fact puts those who represent the principal into a difficult position. How should issues be prioritized? When push comes to shove, where should the trade-offs be made? Are the interests of other constituencies at stake in a particular deal?

Consider this example:

> *As a bargaining agent for the Pet Groomers Union, Local Number 1, located in Anoka, Minnesota, Hugh discovered that he had to represent a diverse set of interests. The local union is primarily concerned with safety issues. "The members want full-body chain mail whenever they have to work on cats," the local's president told him during a briefing. "Have you ever tangled with an 18-pound tomcat with an attitude?"*
>
> *Hugh can see the local union's point, but he also has to consider the larger issues of pay, benefits, and working conditions. If he trades off any of those values in resolving the safety issue for this one group, he'll be setting a precedent that could create problems for other Pet Groomer locals that have different interests.*

There is no easy answer for how to handle a situation such as Hugh's. Politicians face the same problem every day and usually try to solve it by promising to give something to everyone. This is rarely possible in the commercial sphere, where constraints cannot be legislated away.

As discussed in the previous section, the best solution is communication with constituents—communication that aims for consensus regarding priorities. In these instances, the agent has to act as an educator, helping constituents understand external realities. Sometimes the agent must be a coalition builder.

Conflicts of Interest

The third major issue in the principal/agent relationship is the fact that every agent is bound to have a personal agenda, and that agenda may conflict with the principal's agenda. Michael Watkins and Joel Cutcher-Gershenfeld have used the example of sports and entertainment agents to indicate how an agent's personal interest may eclipse his or her clients' interests. "These agents may even court controversy or engage in other behaviors designed to attract future clients—with neutral or negative implications for the present clients they ostensibly represent."[1] Ambitious sports and entertainment agents are not the only representatives who may be tempted to direct negotiations in ways that benefit themselves. Consider a business executive charged with negotiating an important deal. If several constituencies within his company have stakes in the outcome, this executive may be tempted to produce a good result for whichever constituency can best advance his career.

This type of problem is observed repeatedly, and at the very highest levels. CEOs, for example, are, at bottom, agents of shareholders. They are hired to maximize shareholder wealth and are bound by a fiduciary duty to do so. That duty has not, however, prevented many CEOs from awarding themselves with lavish perks or cutting sweetheart retirement deals with corporate boards.

Generally, companies (and shareholders) use incentives to align the interests of agents with their own interests. The idea is simple in concept: The agents only do well if the organizations they represent do well. Bonuses, profit sharing, and stock options are the primary tools of alignment. However, this simple idea is difficult to implement in practice. Watkins and Cutcher-Gershenfeld note that "it is not possible for a principal to design an incentive system that perfectly aligns an agent's interests with her own."[2] Create a pay-for-performance system, and employee-agents will immediately channel their ingenuity into tactics for playing the game in their favor.

Incentives may be imperfect as a tool for controlling agent behavior, but they are better than nothing. When combined with careful oversight and close communication, they help assure that the interests of principals will be adequately represented in negotiations.

Summing Up

- An agent is a person charged with representing the interests of another (a principal) in negotiations with a third party.

- People engage agents to represent them in negotiations when the agent has greater expertise and when they want to reduce the risk of damaging their relationship with the other side.

- Information asymmetries, divided interests, and conflicts of interest are three important problems in the agent/principal relationship.

- Information asymmetry means that one party has more information than the other. If the principal has much more information than the agent, the agent may have a difficult time representing the principal's interests; in the reverse situation, the agent may discover value-creating opportunities that the principal does not understand or appreciate.

- Not every organization is of one mind as to its core interests. This fact puts those who represent the organization into a difficult position.

- Principals face the problem of preventing agents from putting agent interests ahead of their own. Incentive systems that align the agent's interests with those of the principal can help, especially when combined with oversight and communication.

Negotiation Skills

Building Organizational Competence

Key Topics Covered in This Chapter

- *Continuous improvement—learning from every experience*

- *Building organizational capabilities for negotiating*

- *The characteristics of effective negotiators*

MOST BUSINESSES now understand the importance of building core competencies in areas essential to their strategies. For some companies, new product development is an essential core competence; for others, it's marketing or engineering. Many require competence in several fields. These competencies are the mechanisms that make the execution of high-level strategy possible, and they underpin current and future success.

Negotiating is one of the fields in which organizations need substantial competence, yet few think of it as such. As we've pointed out throughout this book, negotiating skills are required for effective interactions between managers and subordinates, between different departments, between companies and their suppliers, customers, and unions, and in many other situations. Competence in these many forums contributes to the overall success of the organization. Thus, organizations—including yours—need to think about how they can improve the negotiating skills of their people. This chapter explains how you can do it.

Continuous Improvement

Managers have embraced process thinking in the past two decades. Process thinking rests on two pillars. The first is that most of the things done within organizations—from handling expense reports to fulfilling orders to developing new products—are the result of processes.

Processes are activities that turn inputs into outputs of higher total value. The second pillar is that processes can be improved. They can be made faster, cheaper, or more effective through analysis, redesign, and the application of learning. Together, these two fundamental tenets are the basis of continuous improvement, one of the most powerful business ideas to emerge in recent times.

Continuous improvement can be applied to just about any process in any industry. Motorola pursued continuous improvement when it adopted Six Sigma Quality as the long-term goal of its manufacturing program, eventually reducing product defects to just a few in every million. Improved product quality has added billions of dollars to Motorola's bottom line over the years.

The concept of continuous improvement has spread to other sectors of the economy and to other activities. Banks have used continuous process improvement to reduce the time needed to approve or reject a loan application from several days to several hours, with no reduction in decision-making quality. Insurance companies have done the same with claim processing. Continuous improvement also applies to the manner in which individuals and organizations handle their negotiations.

When applied to negotiations, the discipline of continuous improvement can develop the effectiveness of an organization's internal capabilities and, over time, improve bottom-line results. So why not apply continuous improvement to the negotiation process? Just imagine how much better off your own organization would be if its negotiations with suppliers, customers, alliance partners, and employees were even 10 percent more effective than they are today. Material costs would be lower. Relationships with customers and partners would be stronger and more profitable. Collaboration among individual employees and departments would reach higher levels, producing major benefits for the organization as a whole. Each of these improvements would certainly find their respective paths to a stronger bottom line.

The first step toward continuous improvement in negotiations is to treat negotiation as a process with a fairly universal set of process steps, like those shown in figure 10-1. Whether a negotiation involves

FIGURE 10 - 1

The Negotiation Process: Learning Capture and Reuse

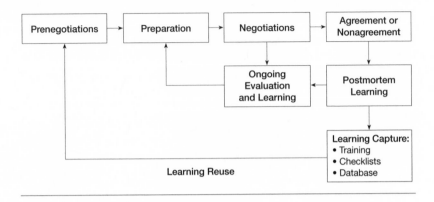

two individuals or multiple participants, and whether it aims to settle a damage dispute or a labor contract, these steps generally apply. Each step in this process represents an opportunity for improvement, and each should be analyzed with that goal in mind.

The second step is to organize to learn from the process as it takes place, and at the conclusion of the negotiation itself. For example, participants should continually evaluate progress during negotiations and revise their tactics as necessary. They should also use what they've learned in one phase of a negotiation to prepare for the next phase. The feedback loop labeled "ongoing evaluation and learning" in the figure represents this activity. And, of course, participants should conduct a postmortem at the conclusion of every negotiation to determine what worked, what didn't work, and how their experiences can be used to improve future negotiating outcomes.

Finally, postmortem learning should be captured in forms that make learning easily disseminated and reusable by future negotiators: training courses, checklists, and databases. Learning capture and reuse is reflected in figure 10-1 through a feedback loop.

As you organize to improve your negotiating processes and capabilities, recognize the need to overcome four key barriers:

- The outcomes of a negotiation are not always clear. For example, the negotiator who negotiates a rock-bottom price with a key supplier may not realize that he or she has soured an important relationship.

- In some cases, the true consequences of a negotiation cannot be measured for many years.

- In learning from the negotiating experience, one cannot always say, "This action produced these results." The presence of many uncontrolled variables makes such certainty impossible.

- Individuals may not have incentives to share their negotiating know-how with others.

Nevertheless, experience, and the learning it produces, can help individual negotiators to improve their performance over time. And lessons distilled from that learning can educate other individuals.

Negotiating as an Organizational Capability

Unfortunately, few companies apply continuous improvement to their negotiations. Nor do they think systematically about their negotiating activities as a whole or of negotiating as a key organizational capability. Instead, they take a situational view, perceiving each negotiation as a separate event with its own goals, tactics, participants, and measures of success. As a consequence, they fail to capture learning for future use. By treating negotiating as an ad hoc activity instead of an organizational capability, they never get better at it—and they often pay a high price at the bargaining table.

An organization can improve its overall negotiating skill and turn that skill into an important capability by heeding the following guidelines:

- Provide training and preparation resources for negotiators.

- Clarify organizational goals and expectations regarding any agreement—and when negotiators should walk away.

- Insist that every negotiating team develop a best alternative to a negotiated agreement (BATNA) and work to improve it.

- Develop mechanisms for capturing and reusing lessons learned from previous negotiations.

- Develop negotiating performance measures and link them to rewards.

Let's consider each of these measures in greater detail.

Provide Training and Resources

In his article "Turning Negotiation into a Corporate Capability," Danny Ertel described how a Mexican bank, Serfin, was faced with the task of renegotiating many loans in the wake of that country's 1994 currency devaluation. "Desperate to improve its negotiation process, the bank decided to take a new tack. It looked for opportunities to standardize and codify its negotiation processes, to impose some management controls, and to change the negotiator's concession-oriented cultures. In short, it set about building a corporate infrastructure for negotiations."[1]

Serfin began with a training curriculum that put its negotiators in real-world positions. It followed up with the technical resources that its "work out" negotiators would need in the field. These helped with pre-negotiating preparation. Finally, it linked its negotiators with the bank's analysts, who were charged, for each particular case, with defining the bank's and the debtor's interests, defining the bank's BATNA, and developing a set of creative options for resolution.

Companies that aim to increase their negotiating capabilities, as this bank did, can likewise provide preparation checklists and access to lessons learned from earlier negotiating experience. They can also help novices gain experience through apprenticeship. Apprentices assigned to more experienced negotiators can participate in actual deals and develop a sense of how things happen. This "sense" is part of the art of negotiating. Good negotiators are people who have learned to recognize threats and opportunities in a background of unimportant clutter. They develop this pattern recognition through experience. Apprenticeships give novices opportunities to develop pattern recognition while freeing them from the risk of making mistakes. The same can be accomplished through the use of case studies and simulations.

Clarify Goals and Expectations

When they begin negotiating with an outside party, negotiators shouldn't have to guess at organizational goals and expectations. They should have clear direction from senior management. For example, if management is concerned with improving profit margins but fails to communicate that goal effectively, its field sales force may be negotiating agreements with customers that discount prices to win new accounts—just the opposite of what management wants. The antidote is for management to be clear in its expectations, and tell its negotiators when it expects them to walk away from a deal. Negotiating goals must be aligned with organizational goals and supported with the right incentives.

Insist That Every Negotiating Team Knows Its BATNA

The concept of best alternative to a negotiated agreement has been discussed throughout this book. A strong BATNA relative to the other side gives negotiators bargaining power. And knowledge of their own BATNA tells negotiators when it's smart to walk away. Companies should insist that their representatives have a clear understanding of their BATNA and that they have explored ways of strengthening their best alternative.

Capture and Reuse Lessons Learned

The idea of capturing experience and reusing it in future analogous situations is an essential part of the now-popular field of knowledge management. Consulting firms, tax accounting firms, and other knowledge-based enterprises have been pioneers of knowledge management—and for very practical reasons. Learning how to solve a knotty business problem or how to apply an ambiguous provision of the tax code is often time-consuming, costly, and subject to error. Knowledge capture and reuse allows these firms to avoid reinventing the wheel. For example, a tax accountant based in New York City is unsure how to treat a financial transaction made by a film producer. A search of her firm's database indicates how colleagues in the Los Angeles office have successfully handled the same type of transaction. The file also includes an opinion letter issued by the Internal Revenue Service. In this example, knowledge capture and reuse improves both productivity and service quality.

Something similar can be obtained when companies are systematic in recording the outcomes of negotiations. As reported by Danny Ertel, one major professional services firm is developing a centralized database to help its project managers negotiate scope-and-fee agreements with clients. "Every time a manager negotiates with a client," he reports, "he or she will now be expected to fill out a brief questionnaire that captures the approaches taken, the results achieved, and the lessons learned."[2] The reports are entered into a database and made available to other project managers as they prepare for upcoming negotiations with clients.

Develop Performance Measures and Link Them to Rewards

You've heard the old saying "Companies get what they measure and reward." Thus, when companies base sales bonuses on revenue instead of operating profits from sales, the sales force has every motive to use costly service perks and other inducements to bring in new customers—many of whom are unprofitable to serve. The same applies to negotiators. When companies reward their negotiators for squeezing the lowest possible price out of suppliers, they enjoy short-term gains at the expense of relationship values. Their negotiators ignore win-win opportunities in favor of the zero-sum game. And suppliers have every reason to leave them in the lurch as soon as they find better partners. Change the measurement and rewards system, and the outcomes will be different.

Thus, management must create alignment between its goals and how it measures and rewards negotiators. Danny Ertel provided *Harvard Business Review* readers with the example of a set of measures used by an engineering and architectural services firm (table 10-1). This firm was less interested in simply booking more business at higher rates and more interested in a broader spectrum of financial and relationship values. Management used those measures to evaluate deal results and negotiator performance; employees used the same measures to prepare for impending negotiations.

In view of this discussion, consider the measures against which your organization evaluates and prepares for negotiations.

TABLE 10-1

A Broad Set of Measures for Evaluating the Success of Negotiations

Relationship	Has the negotiation helped build the kind of relationship that will enable us and our clients to work effectively together over the project's life cycle?
Communication	Do these negotiations help create an environment in which both parties can engage in constructive, problem-solving conversations?
Interests	Does the deal satisfy our interests well at the same time that it satisfies our client's interests to an acceptable level and the interests of relevant third parties to at least a tolerable level?
Options	Have we searched for innovative and efficient solutions with the potential for joint gain?
Legitimacy	Have we used objective criteria to evaluate and select an option that can be justified by both sides?
BATNA	Have we measured the proposed deal against our best alternative to a negotiated agreement? Are we confident that the deal satisfies our interests better than does our best alternative?
Commitment	Have we generated well-planned, realistic, and workable commitments that both sides understand and are prepared to implement?

Source: Adapted from Danny Ertel, "Turning Negotiation into a Corporate Capability," *Harvard Business Review,* May–June 1999, 55.

- Can you even identify your company's measures?

- Are they sufficiently broad?

- Are they used to align the behavior of negotiators with organizational goals?

- Are they used for rewards?

If you answered "no" to any of these questions, start rethinking your current measures.

What Makes an Effective Negotiator?

Everything discussed so far in this chapter has addressed the organizational issues of improving negotiating competence. What we haven't addressed are the characteristics of effective negotiators. The two go hand in hand. Organizational competence is, in fact, the sum of the competence of the organization's individual members—including you.

In ending this chapter—and the book—it's fitting to ask, "What are the characteristics of an effective negotiator?" The answer defines the goals that management should aim for in developing organization-wide capabilities. It also indicates what you should aim for in developing your own tool-kit of skills.

The personal characteristics that make negotiators effective are derived from the topics treated in previous chapters. An effective negotiator

- **Aligns negotiating goals with organizational goals.** An effective negotiator operates within a framework that supports the strategic goals of the organization. This is only possible when those goals are clear. Senior management has a responsibility to communicate goals to everyone from the executive suite to the mail room—including those who negotiate on its behalf. That communication is the best assurance of alignment between goals and employee behaviors—and negotiated outcomes.

- **Prepares thoroughly and uses each negotiating phase to prepare further.** In effective organizations, people come to meetings prepared with facts and proposals. They don't wing it. The people who negotiate for themselves, their departments, and the organization must be equally prepared.

- **Uses negotiating sessions to learn more about the issues at stake and the other side's BATNA and reservation price.** Negotiators, like card players, must often operate in a fog of uncertainty. Advantage generally accrues to the parties who, through preparation and dialogue, gather the information that allows them to penetrate that fog. One's BATNA and reservation price are generally knowable, and the other side's can often be ascertained through effective dialogue and away-from-the-table detective work.

- **Has the mental dexterity to identify the interests of both sides, and the creativity to think of value-creating options that produce win-win situations.** A really good negotiator confronted with what others perceive as a zero-sum game can change that game. He or she can help the other side see the value of sharing information and expanding the universe of value opportunities.

- **Can separate personal issues from negotiating issues.** The accomplished negotiator knows that it is not about him or her—or even about the individuals sitting across the table. This negotiator operates with objective detachment and focuses on producing the best possible outcome.

- **Can recognize potential barriers to agreement.** Barriers aren't always obvious. A skillful negotiator ferrets them out and finds ways to neutralize them.

- **Knows how to form coalitions.** Not every negotiator is dealt a winning hand. The other side often has greater power at the table. A good negotiator, however, knows that a coalition of several weak players can often counter that power. More important, he or she knows how to build such a coalition on a foundation of shared interests.

- **Develops a reputation for reliability and trustworthiness.** The
  most effective negotiations are built on trust. Trust formed
  through one phase of negotiation pays dividends in the next.
  Good negotiators practice ethical behavior. They are as good
  as their words.

With training and experience, you can develop these characteristics
and become an effective negotiator.

Summing Up

It's one thing to develop one's individual negotiating skills. Developing the negotiating skills of an organization at many levels is a very
different challenge, but one with great potential rewards. This chapter explored that challenge from several perspectives.

- The discipline of continuous improvement can develop the effectiveness of an organization's internal capabilities and, over
  time, improve bottom-line results. This same discipline can be
  applied to the negotiation process.

- The first step toward continuous improvement in negotiations
  is to treat negotiation as a process with a fairly universal set of
  process steps: pre-negotiations, preparation, negotiations, agreement or nonagreement, postmortem learning, and learning
  capture. Learning capture feeds back to the next negotiating
  experience. The second step is to organize to learn from the
  process as it takes place, and at the conclusion of the negotiation itself.

- An organization can improve its overall negotiating skill and
  turn that skill into an important capability by doing the following: providing training and preparation for negotiators, clarifying organizational goals and expectations from any agreement
  and clarifying when negotiators should walk away, insisting that
  every negotiating team develop a BATNA and work to improve
  it, developing mechanisms for capturing and reusing lessons

learned from previous negotiations, and developing negotiating performance measures and linking them to rewards.

Because organizational competence is the sum of the competences of an organization's individual members, the chapter concluded with the characteristics of effective negotiators. These define the goals that management should aim for in developing organization-wide capabilities. An effective negotiator

- Aligns negotiating goals with organizational goals

- Prepares thoroughly and uses each negotiating phase to prepare further

- Uses negotiating sessions to learn more about the issues at stake and the other side's BATNA and reservation price

- Has the mental dexterity to identify the interests of both sides, and the creativity to think of value-creating options that produce win–win situations

- Can separate personal issues from negotiating issues

- Can recognize potential barriers to agreement

- Knows how to form coalitions

- Develops a reputation for reliability and trustworthiness

Useful Implementation Tools

This appendix contains several worksheets that can help you as you prepare for and engage in negotiations. You can find these and other tools online at the Harvard Business Essentials Web site: www.elearn ing.hbsp.org/businesstools.

1. **Preparing for a Negotiation.** Use this worksheet to track the outcomes of each step in preparing for a negotiation. (Circle "yes" after all items within a category are completed.)

2. **Identifying Your BATNA.** Complete this worksheet to identify your BATNA (best alternative to a negotiated agreement) and find ways to improve it.

3. **Setting Your Reservation Price.** This is your "walk away" price. Use this worksheet to examine the variables that can determine your reservation price.

4. **Assessing the Other Side's Position and Interests.** How much do you know about the other side? What is their BATNA? What is the least favorable point at which the other side would accept a deal (their reservation price)? Their underlying interests? Use this worksheet to summarize your knowledge of the other side. Examine your findings for key negotiation points.

5. **Authority—Theirs and Yours.** Use this worksheet to determine and confirm the authority level you have and the authority level of the person or persons with whom you will be negotiating, so that you can plan accordingly.

EXHIBIT A-1

Preparing for a Negotiation

Have you . . . Thought through what would be a good outcome?	**Yes**
What do you hope to accomplish through the negotiation?	
What would the best result look like?	
What outcomes would not be palatable?	
Why would these outcomes not be palatable?	

. . . Assessed your needs and interests?		**Yes**
What you must have	**What you would like to have**	
1.	1.	
2.	2.	
3.	3.	

. . . Identified and improved (if possible) your BATNA?	**Yes**
What is your best alternative to a negotiated agreement? *(See the "Identifying Your BATNA" worksheet.)*	
What are the ways you might be able to improve your BATNA?	

. . . Determined your reservation price? *(See the "Setting Your Reservation Price" worksheet.)*	**Yes**
What is it?	

. . . Evaluated the trade-offs between issues and interests?		**Yes**
Issues you care most about?	**Terms you care most about?**	
1.	1.	
2.	2.	
3.	3.	

EXHIBIT A - 1

Preparing for a Negotiation

. . . Assessed the other side's people, BATNA, and position? *(See the "Assessing the Other Side's Position and Interests" worksheet.)* The people for the other side:	**Yes**
Their business circumstances:	
What, specifically, they want from this deal:	
The value this deal has for them:	
The availability of a replacement deal:	
. . . Anticipated the authority issue? Summarize . . . *(See the "Authority—Theirs and Yours" worksheet.)* Your understanding of the level of authority of representative(s) at the table for the other side:	**Yes**
The kind of deal you are authorized to make:	
. . . Gathered the external standards and criteria relevant to the negotiation? *(In this deal, what standards and criteria are considered "fair and reasonable"?)* External standards:	**Yes**
Relevant criteria:	
. . . Prepared for flexibility? *(Is there linkage between issues? If "yes," which ones?)*	**Yes**

Source: HMM Negotiating.

EXHIBIT A-2

Identifying Your BATNA

<table>
<tr><td colspan="2">

1. What are your alternatives to a negotiated agreement? Identify your best alternative.

Make a list of what your alternatives will be if the negotiation ends without agreement.
</td></tr>
<tr><td>1.</td></tr>
<tr><td>2.</td></tr>
<tr><td>3.</td></tr>
<tr><td>4.</td></tr>
<tr><td>**Review the list. Which of these alternatives would be best?**</td></tr>
<tr><td>

2. What could improve your BATNA? Consider . . .
</td></tr>
<tr><td>Are there any better arrangements you can make with other suppliers/partners/customers?</td></tr>
<tr><td>Is there any way to remove or alter any constraint that makes your current BATNA bad? What? How?</td></tr>
<tr><td>Is there any way to change the terms you bring to the table that could improve your BATNA? What? How?</td></tr>
<tr><td>

3. Write what your "new" BATNA will be, if you succeed in improving it.
</td></tr>
</table>

Source: HMM Negotiating.

EXHIBIT A-3

Setting Your Reservation Price

<table>
<tr><td>

1. Explore the variables that affect your reservation, or "away," position.

</td></tr>
<tr><td>

What is the value to you of the deal on the table?

</td></tr>
<tr><td>

How does this compare to the value of your BATNA?

</td></tr>
<tr><td>

What other values or stakeholders need to be considered?

</td></tr>
<tr><td>

If there is a dollar number involved in the negotiation, what is the lowest amount that you can consider?

</td></tr>
<tr><td>

What are the minimum non-dollar terms that you would consider?

</td></tr>
<tr><td>

2. Evaluate the trade-offs between issues and interests.

</td></tr>
<tr><td>

Which issue(s) or term(s) do you care most about?

</td></tr>
<tr><td>

Are any of these issues or terms linked? *(That is, does more or less of what you want on one issue give you more or less flexibility on any of the others?)*

</td></tr>
<tr><td>

How much of what you want on one issue or term would you trade off against another?

</td></tr>
<tr><td>

Are there different package deals that would be equivalent in value to you?

</td></tr>
<tr><td>

3. Articulate the parameters of your reservation price.
(The resulting terms or price create the context for you to evaluate alternative proposals.)

</td></tr>
</table>

Source: HMM Negotiating.

EXHIBIT A-4

Assessing the Other Side's Position and Interests

To learn as much as you can about the other side's interest and concerns, have you . . .	Yes	No
1. Contacted sources within the industry?		
2. Checked potentially relevant business publications?		
3. Reviewed their annual reports (and public filings)?		
4. Asked questions informally of the negotiator or others within the company?		
5. Imagined what your interests, preferences, and needs would be if you were in their position?		
Assess the other side's BATNA. What do you know . . .		
About the other side's business circumstances? How strong is their financial performance?		
What is their strategy?		
What are their key corporate initiatives?		
What competitive pressures do they face?		
About the value this deal has to them? How important is this deal to the other side at this time?		
Is it necessary for them to meet a larger objective? *(Describe the objective.)*		
About the availability of a replacement deal? Is what you offer easy to find elsewhere?		
Can it be obtained in time to meet their deadlines?		
Have they already obtained bids from or initiated informal negotiations with anyone else?		
Consider the terms the other side would like to see for the deal.		
What broader business objectives would the other side like to see served by this deal?		
What terms of this deal could hamper their business growth?		
What terms might you offer that would benefit the other side (at a low cost to you)?		

Source: HMM Negotiating.

EXHIBIT A-5

Authority—Theirs and Yours

Their authority: *(Learn as much as possible about the individuals on the other side.)*
1. Who will be at the negotiating table?
2. What are the formal titles and areas of responsibility of the person(s) with whom you will be negotiating?
3. What are their ages/how long have they been with the company/what other relevant experience do they have?
4. How is the company structured? *(Is it hierarchical, with significant decision-making powers centered at the top, or is it relatively decentralized?)*
5. How are the negotiators viewed within the organization? *(Are they generally respected and listened to, or not? Rely on contacts outside the organization, if available.)*
6. What are their other interests outside of work? *(i.e., sports, hobbies, volunteer interests, political orientation, children?)*
Your authority: *(Confirm in as much detail as possible.)*   **What kind of a deal are you authorized to make?** *(Complete as appropriate.)*
Only a predetermined deal for which committee approval has been obtained? *(If yes, describe. If you can also negotiate something "better" beyond the predetermined deal, what does the committee consider "better"?)*
Only a deal that meets certain objectives? *(What are the objectives? Do you have freedom to structure the deal in the best way you can?)*
Would the committee prefer that you bring a deal back for formal review and approval?
Is your authority limited on dollar issues but not on other creative options without significant financial implications?
Are you authorized to provide information about your company's needs, interests, and preferences if the other side engages in a good-faith, reciprocal exchange?

Source: HMM Negotiating.

Notes

Chapter 1

1. "Win-Win with Mark Gordon," *Harvard Management Communication Letter*, March 1999, 1–3.
2. Ibid.
3. Jim Camp, *Start with No* (New York: Crown, 2002), 4–6.
4. This section is adapted from the Negotiating module of Harvard ManageMentor, an online service of Harvard Business School Publishing.

Chapter 2

1. David A. Lax and James K. Sebenius, *The Manager as Negotiator* (New York: Free Press, 1986), 57–58.
2. Danny Ertel, "Turning Negotiation into a Corporate Capability," *Harvard Business Review*, May–June 1999, 55.

Chapter 3

1. The nine steps are adapted from the Negotiating module of Harvard ManageMentor, an online service of Harvard Business School Publishing.
2. Jim Camp, *Start with No* (New York: Crown, 2002), 22.
3. Deborah M. Kolb and Judith Williams, "Breakthrough Bargaining," *Harvard Business Review*, February 2001, 93.

Chapter 4

1. Adapted from the Negotiating module of Harvard ManageMentor, an online service of Harvard Business School Publishing.
2. Deborah M. Kolb and Judith Williams, "Breakthrough Bargaining," *Harvard Business Review*, February 2001, 90.
3. Max H. Bazerman and Margaret A. Neale, *Negotiating Rationally* (New York: Free Press, 1992), 23.
4. Ibid., 31.

5. Marjorie Corman Aaron, "The Right Frame: Managing Meaning and Making Proposals," *Harvard Management Communication Letter,* September 1999, 1–4.

6. Michael Watkins, "Rethinking 'Preparation' in Negotiations," Class Note 9-801-286 (Boston: Harvard Business School Publishing, revised October 9, 2001), 11.

Chapter 5

1. Adapted from the Negotiating module of Harvard ManageMentor, an online service of Harvard Business School Publishing.

Chapter 6

1. David McCollough, *John Adams* (New York: Simon & Schuster, 2001), 366.

2. Diane Coutu, "Negotiating Without a Net," *Harvard Business Review,* October 2002, 50.

3. Michael D. Watkins, "Diagnosing and Overcoming Barriers to Agreement," Class Note 9-800-333 (Boston: Harvard Business School Publishing, revised May 8, 2000), 15.

4. Gary Hamel and Yves Doz, *Alliance Advantage* (Boston: Harvard Business School Press, 1998), 14.

Chapter 7

1. Max H. Bazerman and Margaret A. Neale, *Negotiating Rationally* (New York: Free Press, 1992), 10.

2. David Bunnell with Richard Luecke, *The eBay Phenomenon* (New York: John Wiley & Sons, 2000), 48.

3. Irving Janus, *Groupthink: Psychological Studies of Policy Decisions and Fiascos* (Boston: Houghton Mifflin, 1982), 9.

4. Bazerman and Neale, *Negotiating Rationally,* 116.

Chapter 8

1. John Kotter, *Power and Influence* (New York: Free Press, 1985), 40.

2. Danny Ertel, "Turning Negotiation into a Corporate Capability," *Harvard Business Review,* May–June 1999, 55.

3. Ibid., 62.

4. Ibid., 64.

Chapter 9

1. Michael Watkins and Joel Cutcher-Gershenfeld, "Representing Others in Negotiations," paper presented to the Academy of Management,

August 1997, and reprinted in *Negotiating on Behalf of Others: Advice to Lawyers, Business Executives, Sports Agents, Diplomats, Politicians, and Everybody Else,* eds. Robert H. Mnookin, Lawrence E. Susskind, and Pacey C. Foster (New York: Sage, 1999).

    2. Ibid.

Chapter 10

    1. Danny Ertel, "Turning Negotiation into a Corporate Capability," *Harvard Business Review,* May–June 1999, 55.

    2. Ibid., 57.

Glossary

AGENT A person charged with representing the interests of another in negotiations with a third party.

ANCHORING An attempt to establish an initial position around which negotiations will make adjustments.

BATNA Acronym for "best alternative to a negotiated agreement." Knowing your BATNA means knowing the options of what you will do or what will happen if you do not reach agreement in the negotiation at hand.

BLUFFING A tactic in which one party in a negotiation indicates that it may be willing to do or accept something that it actually has no intention of following through on. For example, a tenant may bluff that he will not renew his lease unless certain improvements are made to his office space.

COMPLIANCE TRANSPARENCY The ability to monitor compliance with the terms of an agreement from the outside.

DIE-HARD BARGAINERS People for whom every negotiation is a battle.

DISTRIBUTIVE NEGOTIATION A type of negotiation in which the parties compete over the distribution of a fixed pool of value. Here, any gain by one party represents a loss to the other. Popularly referred to as a *zero-sum negotiation* or *win-lose* negotiation.

EXPLODING OFFER An offer with an expiration date.

GROUPTHINK A mode of thinking that engages members of a cohesive "in" group. Groupthink is driven by consensus and tends to override the motivation to realistically appraise alternative courses of action.

INFORMATION ASYMMETRY A situation in which one party has more information than another.

INSECURE AGREEMENT   An agreement that is hedged or more narrow or limited than it would otherwise be because of lack of trust between the negotiating parties.

INTEGRATIVE NEGOTIATION   A type of negotiation in which the parties cooperate to achieve maximum mutual benefit in an agreement. Long-term partnerships and collaborations between colleagues are often characterized by integrative negotiation. More popularly known as a *win-win* negotiation.

INTERESTS   The goals underlying a party's negotiating position.

IRRATIONAL ESCALATION   Per Max Bazerman and Margaret Neale, continuing a previously selected course of action beyond what rational analysis would recommend.

MULTIPARTY NEGOTIATIONS   Negotiations that involve more than two parties. Such negotiations can differ significantly from two-party negotiations, especially when coalitions—alliances among parties that wield less power separately than they do together—form among the parties.

MULTIPHASE TRANSACTIONS   Negotiations that will be implemented in phases, or that have the prospect of subsequent involvement in the future. The context of the negotiations allows parties to negotiate based on follow-through and continuing communication.

NATURAL COALITION   A group of allies who share a broad range of common interests.

NEGOTIATOR'S DILEMMA   The tension caused by the negotiator's attempt to balance competitive strategies—trying to discern when to compete where interests conflict, and when to create value by exchanging the information that leads to mutually advantageous options.

PARTISAN PERCEPTION   The psychological phenomenon that causes people to perceive truth with a built-in bias in their own favor or toward their own point of view. For example, both teams in a baseball game may perceive that the umpire was unfair to their side.

POSITIONS   What the parties in a negotiation are asking for—in other words, their demands.

PROCESSES   Activities that turn inputs into outputs of higher total value.

RESERVATION PRICE   The least favorable point at which a party would accept a negotiated deal. The reservation price is derived from, but is not usually the same thing as, the BATNA. Also known as *walk-away*.

SINGLE-ISSUE COALITION A group whose members may differ on other issues, but who nevertheless unite (though often for different reasons) to support or block a certain particular issue.

STRATEGY A planned sequence of how one is going to approach a negotiation, including what the negotiator will offer and ask for (give and get).

TACTICS The specific methods for implementing a strategy.

TRADE OFF To substitute or bargain one issue for another; this tactic is often used in sales negotiations.

WALK-AWAY See *reservation price*.

WIGGLE ROOM The flexibility that may exist in a particular offer, whether it has to do with money or time frame. If you have no wiggle room, you should strongly convey the message that this is your best offer.

WIN-LOSE See *distributive negotiation*.

WIN-WIN See *integrative negotiation*.

WINNER'S CURSE After a deal has been reached, the nagging conviction that one could have negotiated a more favorable deal.

ZERO-SUM NEGOTIATION See *distributive negotiation*.

ZOPA Acronym for "zone of possible agreement." This is the area in which a potential deal can take place. Each party's reservation price defines one of the boundaries of the ZOPA. The ZOPA itself exists, if at all, in the overlap between the parties' reservation prices.

For Further Reading

Notes and Articles

Conger, Jay. "The Necessary Art of Persuasion." *Harvard Business Review* OnPoint Enhanced Edition. Boston: Harvard Business School Publishing, 2000. Persuasion is a major part of any negotiation. This article explains the four essential elements of persuasion: (1) establishing credibility, (2) finding common ground, (3) providing vivid evidence for your position, and (4) connecting emotionally with your audience.

Ertel, Danny. "Turning Negotiation into a Corporate Capability." *Harvard Business Review* OnPoint Enhanced Edition. Boston: Harvard Business School Publishing, 2000. Every company today exists in a complex web of relationships formed, one at a time, through negotiation. Purchasing and outsourcing contracts are negotiated with vendors. Marketing arrangements are negotiated with distributors. Product development agreements are negotiated with joint venture partners. Taken together, the thousands of negotiations a typical company engages in have an enormous effect on both its strategy and its bottom line. But few companies think systematically about their negotiating activities as a whole. Instead they take a situational view, perceiving each negotiation to be a separate event with its own goals, tactics, and measures of success. Coordinating them all seems an overwhelming and impracticable job. In reality, the author argues, it is neither. He presents four broad changes in practice and perspective that, taken together, will let companies establish closer, more creative relationships with suppliers, customers, and other partners.

Harvard Business School Publishing. "How to Get What You Want." *Harvard Management Communication Letter*, March 2000. How do you improve your chances while negotiating? Start by understanding how you can help or hurt your competition, and how they can help or hurt you.

Answer these three questions: (1) What do you want? (2) Why should your competition negotiate with you? and (3) What are your alternatives? Includes dos and don'ts for navigating negotiation sessions.

Kolb, Deborah M., and Judith Williams. "Breakthrough Bargaining." *Harvard Business Review* OnPoint Enhanced Edition. Boston: Harvard Business School Publishing, 2001. Unspoken, subtle elements in the bargaining process—the "shadow negotiation"—can set the tone for any negotiation. The authors provide three kinds of strategies for successful bargaining: (1) Power moves show the other side that it's in their interest to negotiate with you, (2) process moves influence how others view the negotiation, and (3) appreciative moves alter the tone of the interaction so that the parties can have a more collaborative exchange.

Sebenius, James K. "Six Habits of Merely Effective Negotiators." *Harvard Business Review* OnPoint Enhanced Edition. Boston: Harvard Business School Publishing, 2002. Even seasoned negotiators fall prey at times to six all-too-common mistakes that keep them from solving the right negotiation problem. These mistakes include neglecting the other party's problem, letting price eclipse other interests, letting positions eclipse interests, searching too hard for common ground, neglecting no-deal alternatives, and failing to correct for skewed vision. The author contrasts good and bad negotiating practice, drawing from fifty years of research and analysis.

Shell, Richard. "When Is It Legal to Lie in Negotiations?" *Sloan Management Review* 32, no. 3 (spring 1991). This short and clearly written article sets forth the legal framework for understanding when and why lying will get you into trouble in negotiation. Using case examples, it provides guidance for those uncomfortable with the sometimes fuzzy distinctions between lying and bluffing, puffing, or not telling.

Williams, Monci J. "Don't Avoid Conflicts—Manage Them." *Harvard Management Update,* July 1997. Regardless of our hierarchical position in an organization, most of us believe it is expedient, and therefore preferable, to avoid conflict. Research indicates, however, that avoiding conflict may hinder managers in achieving their goals. To manage conflict successfully you need to understand the difference between positions and underlying needs. You should also understand the other party's position before asserting your own. By concentrating on common interests and knowing your own "hot buttons," you and your partners in conflict can arrive at an optimal solution rather than a simple compromise.

Books

Bazerman, Max, and Margaret Neale. *Negotiating Rationally.* New York: Free Press, 1992. Professors Bazerman and Neale bring their psychologists' lens to this work on negotiation theory and practice. Their bottom-line advice is much like that in *Getting to Yes* and *The Manager as Negotiator* (see entries below), but they also weave in explanations and insights from psychological research and literature.

Camp, Jim. *Start with No.* New York: Crown, 2002. A contrarian approach to personal and business negotiation problems. Of particular interest is the author's critique of the conventional win–win mentality advocated by many other authors and consultants. Camp believes that this mentality results in win–lose outcomes.

Fisher, Roger, William Ury, and Bruce Patton. *Getting to Yes: Negotiating Agreement Without Giving In.* 2d ed. New York: Penguin, 1991. The original 1981 edition had a tremendous impact on everything from international politics to professional schools and executive education courses in negotiation. *Getting to Yes* sets up a polemic between "positional bargaining" and "principled negotiation." The heart of the book articulates a basic prescriptive framework for "principled negotiation" or "negotiation on the merits": Separate the people from the problem; focus on interests, not positions; invent options for mutual gain; and insist on objective criteria.

Harvard Business School Publishing. *Harvard Business Review on Negotiation and Conflict Resolution.* Boston: Harvard Business School Publishing, 1999. This collection of *Harvard Business Review* articles offers the best thinking on negotiation practice and conflict management from the Review.

Harvard Business School Publishing. *The Manager's Guide to Negotiation and Conflict Resolution.* Harvard Management Update Collection. Boston: Harvard Business School Publishing, 2000. One of the most difficult issues managers must deal with every day is negotiation in the broadest sense. Whether it's negotiating for a raise, or with your colleagues to promote a project, or more formally with other companies to find ways to work together, this essential interpersonal task produces anxiety and stress in most of us. This set of articles hits many key bases.

Lax, David A., and James K. Sebenius. *The Manager as Negotiator.* New York: Free Press, 1986. This book brings together scholarship and experience in a useful way. It covers not only the basics that any manager, attorney, or diplomat would need to know, but also discusses negotiations in situations of special interest to managers: negotiating in hierarchies and in networks, with internal and external entities, and so forth.

Mnookin, Robert H., Lawrence E. Susskind, and Pacey C. Foster, eds. *Negotiating on Behalf of Others: Advice to Lawyers, Business Executives, Sports Agents, Diplomats, Politicians, and Everybody Else.* New York: Sage Publications, 1999. This specialized and somewhat academic book offers a framework for understanding the complexity and outcomes of negotiations by agents. The authors include among agents the following: legislators, diplomats, salespersons, sports agents, attorneys, and committee chairs. A book of chapters contributed by leading scholars and practitioners, it examines five arenas in detail: labor-management relations, international diplomacy, sports agents, legislative process, and agency law.

Watkins, Michael. *Breakthrough Negotiations*. New York: John Wiley & Sons, 2002. This excellent book presents principles that apply to business negotiations, and tools for achieving good results. Of particular interest are the author's approaches to diagnosing a situation, building coalitions, and creating strategic alliances.

Zeckhauser, Richard J., Ralph L. Keeney, and James K. Sebenius, eds. *Wise Choices: Decisions, Games, and Negotiations*. Boston: Harvard Business School Press, 1996. Leading scholars in economics, psychology, statistics, and decision theory grapple with strategic uncertainty and the question of how to make good decisions. The papers in this collection address topics such as individual decision making under uncertainty, games of strategy in which one player's actions directly influence another's welfare, and the process of forging negotiated agreements.

Other Information Sources

Fisher, Roger, William Ury, and Bruce Patton. *Getting to Yes! Video Workshop on Negotiation*. Boston: Harvard Business School Publishing, 1991. Videocassette. This video workshop is the next best thing to having Roger Fisher as your personal negotiation trainer and coach. It brings Fisher's work to life and makes it easy to apply to your own situations. You'll see more than a dozen vignettes that vividly illustrate how to turn adversarial negotiations into mutual problem solving. The workshop gives you everything you need to help you and your managers become more powerful negotiators. Seven video segments take you step by step through the key elements of successful negotiation and act as a springboard for role play.

eLearning Programs

Harvard Business School Publishing. *Influencing and Motivating Others*. Boston: Harvard Business School Publishing, 2001. Online program. Have you ever noticed how some people seem to have a natural ability to stir people to action? *Influencing and Motivating Others* provides actionable lessons on getting better results from direct reports (influencing performance), greater cooperation from your peers (lateral leadership), and stronger support from your own boss and senior management (persuasion). Managers will learn the secrets of "lateral leadership" (leading peers), negotiation and persuasion skills, and how to distinguish between effective and ineffective motivation methods. Through interactive cases, expert guidance, and activities for immediate application at work, this program helps managers assess their ability to effectively persuade others, measure motivation skills, and enhance employee performance.

Harvard Business School Publishing. *Yes! The Online Negotiator.* Boston: Harvard Business School Publishing, 2000. Online program. Based on the techniques developed by world-renowned negotiation expert Roger Fisher and the Harvard Negotiation Project and detailed in the best-seller *Getting to Yes,* this program helps you build strategies for effective negotiation and conflict resolution. You'll negotiate in realistic scenarios, see the consequences of your choices play out, and receive coaching, feedback, and expert advice from Roger Fisher and other experts. *Yes! The Online Negotiator* includes three interactive scenarios: buying a house, acquiring a company, and making a sale.

Index

About the Subject Adviser

Associate Professor **MICHAEL WATKINS** does research on negotiation and leadership. He is the coauthor of *Right from the Start: Taking Charge in a New Leadership Role* (HBS Press, 1999) and the author of *Taking Charge in Your New Leadership Role: A Workbook* (HBS Publishing, 2001), both of which examine how new leaders coming into senior management positions should spend their first six months on the job. He recently coauthored *Winning the Influence Game: What Every Business Leader Should Know About Government* (Wiley, 2001), which provides a framework for analyzing the impact of government on business strategy, as well as tools and techniques for organizing to influence government, and *Breakthrough International Negotiation: How Great Negotiators Transformed the World After the Cold War* (with Susan Rosegrant, Jossey-Bass, 2001). His newest book, *Breakthrough Business Negotiation: A Toolbox for Managers,* was published in April 2002.

About the Writer

RICHARD LUECKE is the writer of several books in the Harvard Business Essentials series. Based in Salem, Massachusetts, Mr. Luecke has authored or developed over thirty books and dozens of articles on a wide range of business subjects. He has an M.B.A. from the University of St. Thomas.

Need smart, actionable management advice?

Look no further than your desktop.

Harvard ManageMentor®, a popular online performance support tool from Harvard Business School Publishing, brings how-to guidance and advice to your desktop, ready when you need it, on a host of issues critical to your work.

Heading up a new team? Resolving a conflict between employees? Preparing a make-or-break presentation for a client? Setting next year's budget? Harvard ManageMentor®Online delivers answers and advice on 33 topics right to your desktop—any time, all the time, just in time.

- Downloadable modules on 28 essential topics allow you to build a personal management resource center right on your computer

- Practical tips, tools, checklists, and resources help you enhance productivity and performance now

- Advice from seasoned experts in finance, communications, teamwork, coaching and more—accessible with a few mouse clicks

- Multiple language versions available

Go to **http://www.harvardmanagementor.com/demo** today to try out two complimentary Harvard ManageMentor® (HMM) Online topics.

Individual topic modules are available for $14.95 each, or you can order the complete HMM Online program (33 topics in all) for $129. Corporate site licenses are also available. For more information or to order, call 800.795.5200 (outside the U.S. and Canada: 617.783.7888) or visit www.harvardmanagementor.com/demo.

HARVARD
ManageMentor®
An online resource for
managers in a hurry